I Am
WHAT
I Am

Mary Ann Pruitt

ISBN 978-1-0980-5059-7 (paperback)
ISBN 978-1-0980-5060-3 (digital)

Copyright © 2021 by Mary Ann Pruitt

All rights reserved. No part of this publication may be reproduced, distributed, or transmitted in any form or by any means, including photocopying, recording, or other electronic or mechanical methods without the prior written permission of the publisher. For permission requests, solicit the publisher via the address below.

Christian Faith Publishing, Inc.
832 Park Avenue
Meadville, PA 16335
www.christianfaithpublishing.com

Scriptures marked KJV are taken from the KING JAMES VERSION (KJV): KING JAMES VERSION, public domain.

Printed in the United States of America

1

Miss Ann

Everyone called her Miss Ann. She was my great-grandmother. I never had the privilege of meeting her, but I have been told of stories about her, some good, some bad. I would like to share these stories that I was told. She was born on December 16, 1869, to George and Martha Craig. She was the eldest of three children: a brother Bud and another brother George who died when he was just a baby. When Ann was about nine or ten years old, her mother, Martha, died; and her daddy was having a real hard time trying to take care of her and her brother Bud.

There was a family who lived not very far from them. Their names were Mr. and Mrs. Sorrles. They were good people and well respected. They asked George, Ann's daddy, if they could help by taking Ann home with them, and he agreed, and she went home with Mr. and Mrs. Sorrles. They took real good care of her. They loved her and treated her as if she were their own child. They gave her what she needed, and she had a good life with them for a long time. But she missed her daddy and her brother. One day she told Mr. and Mrs. Sorrles that she wanted to go back home, but they did not want her to go. They loved her so much, and they offered her a horse and saddle to stay with them. But she insisted on going back. Her daddy had remarried. This took place in the year 1880. He worked as a brickmason. So Ann soon went back home.

When she was maybe fifteen, she met a young man. His name was Doak Anderson. It was like love at first sight, and on December 3, 1885, they got married and were very happy. About a year later,

Ann gave birth to a baby girl, and they named her Lilly Elizabeth. They bought themselves a little farm. It was about six miles from a small town called Lewisburg. It was a little place they worked real hard. They had a few cows and chickens. They worked a garden and grew most of their food.

About three years went by, and Ann gave birth to a son, and they named him Paul. Another three years later, she gave birth to another son, and they named him Jim. Everything was going real good for them. They worked together. Raising their children, they were well respected. They had a good name. The little house that they lived in was very small, maybe three rooms. Ann was a little woman, about 5'2" tall, and weighed about 110 pounds. I was told this, and I have pictures of her that bear this to be true. She had real long light-brown hair, and she kept it platted and pinned up.

I would like to have known her. I called her Grand Maw. I was named after her. I was told that she was a great cook and that she loved to cook and that she also liked to sew. She could take a newspaper and cut a dress pattern out of it and make a dress. It just came naturally for her. She had an old washpot in the backyard, and she would go out there and build a fire around that pot and put water in it, and in a little while, that water would start boiling. She would wash their clothes in a washtub using a rubboard, and then she would throw those clothes in that pot and let them boil for a while. Then she would take them out of the pot and rinse them in another tub and then hang them out on the line to dry. Grand Maw loved taking care of her family.

Everything Was Going Good

Grand Maw and Grandpa Doak would get up early every morning and begin their daily chores. They burned kerosene lamps for light. They could not afford electricity. I was told that Grand Maw would get a tin can and pack a lot of old rags in it, and she would pour oil on it and light it. She called it a burning lamp. It gave a little more light than the kerosene lamps did. She also cooked on a woodstove. They would have to go out and cut wood to put in the stove, and also Grand Maw would go out in the yard a lot of times and catch a chicken and wring its head off. She would dip it into a bucket of hot water, and then she would pick the feathers off it and dress it and cook it for her family. She would also kill and dress chickens for other people in the community, and they would pay her for them.

Grandpa Doak would do odd jobs for people. They would do what they could to make as much money as they could to support their family and pay for their home. Grand Maw would help people sometimes with their housework, and they would pay her, but they continued to work their little farm. They milked cows. Grand Maw had a wood churn, and she would put milk in that old churn. She would sit down in a chair and churn until butter would come to the top of the milk, and then she would skim the butter off. They had homemade butter and buttermilk. They got themselves a horse and buggy, and sometimes they would ride to the store. There was an old store about four or maybe five miles from where they lived in a little place called Belfast, and they would put the children in the buggy, and they would ride. It took a while to get there.

Things were tough sometimes, but they trusted and believed in God to make a way and to supply all their needs. Their children were growing, and they went to school. The little schoolhouse was a one-room school. It was about three miles from where they lived. Grand Maw and Grandpa were very happy. They loved each other and their children.

Things Began to Go Bad

A lot of time went by. Lilly, the eldest of the children, was the age of maybe thirteen, and Paul was ten and Jim seven. Everything was still real good for them until one day Grand Maw began to get sick. I was told that the sickness was in her stomach. She began having a lot of pain, and it did not go away. She got worse, and in those days, the doctor would go to people's houses. I am sure that Grandpa rode his horse to town and told the doctor about Grand Maw's sickness, and the doctor came to their house to see her. Whatever he did to try to help her, it didn't do any good at all. She just kept getting worse.

I do not remember being told the doctor's name, but he came and told her that she would have to have surgery and when this would take place. I was told that five doctors came to their house and performed the surgery, and whatever was wrong, they had to put tubes in her stomach to drain out the infection. Grand Maw almost died. Her pain was almost unbearable. She could hardly stand it, and the doctors gave her morphine to take to help the pain. She could not sleep at night. Grandpa and the children had to sit up with her. They did not know what to do. Her pain was so bad that she would holler and scream, and that would make them afraid.

Grandpa Doak would have to cook for the children, and he also had to do the housework. Lilly would help do some things, and Paul and Jim would do what they could. This went on for a long time, and they were tired. What Grandpa did was a bad mistake. He began giving Grand Maw more of the morphine than what she was supposed to take to calm her down. So she would stop hollering after a period. Grand Maw began to recover from the surgery, but she became addicted to the morphine. She became indifferent, and it was real hard for her family to get along with her. She would become angry when she did not have the morphine. Her family did not know what to do for her. When she could get ten cents or maybe fifteen cents, she would walk to Belfast to get some morphine.

The store in Belfast carried a lot of things. It was not just food, but they carried shoes and a lot of clothes like shirts and overalls. In those days, people could buy a few drugs there, and morphine was one of them. Grand Maw had become desperate for the drug. Things were getting tough, and money was real short. There were a lot of times that Grandpa didn't have the money to get the morphine. Grand Maw's addiction had got out of control. She felt like she had to have this drug somehow. I am sure that Grandpa and the children would wonder what was going to take place next. Grandpa would go out and work in the field with help from the children. Grand Maw would do her housework and help in the field and with whatever had to be done when she felt good, but when she didn't have the morphine, she could not do anything.

Things Got Worse

Grand Maw would look in Grandpa's pockets to see if he had any money. If he did, she would take it and walk to get the drug. Grand Maw had a real bad problem, and things had changed so much. Nothing was the same anymore. She was not trying to do anything to get off the morphine. She got even worse. She was so desperate that she began taking feathers out of the pillows and selling them. In those days, they had feather pillows and feather beds, and the store and people who lived in the community would buy them. Grand Maw had real long hair, and she would cut some of her hair off and sell it to some of the ladies in the community. They would buy her hair to put on the back of their head to make their hair look fuller.

Grand Maw started going off from home. She would just walk off, and she would stay for a long time. Her family didn't know where she was, and then she would come back. Grand Maw's actions were different. She would get angry often, and there were times when Grand Maw would go in the kitchen and cook something special for the children. She would make tea cakes. I have been told that Grand Maw could make some of the best tea cakes.

Time was going by. Grandpa and the children were so worried about Grand Maw. They did not know how to help her. All they could do was to pray and trust God to take care of her and to help her and to keep her safe because the situation was so bad.

Desperate People Do Desperate Things

There was a family who lived nearby, maybe about a mile or two down the road from where Grand Maw and Grandpa lived, and there were times that Grand Maw would be walking maybe to the store, and she would meet some of these people and talk with them. She began talking with this man, and at the beginning, it was friendship, but it was not too long until it went a lot further. Grand Maw was desperate. She was willing to do whatever she could do to get some money to buy some morphine, so she had a relationship with this man, and she became pregnant. This took place in the year 1899, and in June 1900, she gave birth to a brown-skinned baby girl. She named her Mary. The father of this baby was a black man, and in those days, things were so much different than they are today. If a white woman did this, she was rejected and treated as an outcast, and this is what the community did when people would see Grand Maw's new baby girl. They would say Ann had a black baby.

Grand Maw did not talk about all of this to anyone. I am sure when she was pregnant with her baby, she wondered if her husband was the father or the black man, but she took real good care of her baby. People from all around talked real bad about her. They turned their backs on her and would not have anything to do with her. The same people who once admired and respected Grand Maw would not go around her. Grandpa did not know what to do or what to think, but he stayed with Grand Maw and helped her in every way that he could. He treated little Mary the same as he did his other children. He accepted her as his own child. Grand Maw was still taking morphine when she could get it. The children—Lilly, Paul, and Jim—didn't know what to do, but they didn't talk about it. They just loved her anyway.

Grand Maw was sick a lot because of her addiction. Everything was extremely bad. Nobody would help them. Racism was real bad in those days. Grandpa was still working real hard. As time went by, it was a real struggle. Clothes to wear became a problem for all of them, but they all loved one another. All they had was one another, and they stuck together. Through God's grace and mercy, they made it.

In the year 1902, little Mary was two years old. Lilly was sixteen and met a young man. Where he lived was not far from where Grand Maw and Grandpa lived. His name was James Wright. They dated for a short time, and then they got married, and they lived in the same area of Grand Maw and Grandpa. They didn't have much of anything. James didn't work very much. He would do little jobs sometimes for different people.

When it was winter, it was awful for all of them. Grandpa would cut wood to burn in the old fireplace to keep them warm. Grand Maw's old woodstove had what they called a warming closet on the top of it, and she would put bread in there to keep it warm.

I was told that sometimes they only had a little bread to eat. There were a lot of walnut trees around in the country, and they would go out and pick up walnuts and take the kernels out of them and give them to the children. They would get so cold when they did this that their feet and their hands were almost frozen. When spring and summer came, there were a lot of blackberries in the area, and Grand Maw and Grandpa and the children would go and pick blackberries. Sometimes Grand Maw would make pies with the berries when she was not sick.

Time was going by. People were still talking I was told that there were times that the children went to bed hungry. Things were very hard. Grandpa was working all that he could to support his family. In the year 1904, he bought fifty more acres of land from some of the neighbors. He was trying with all his heart. Grand Maw's family had never experienced seeing anyone suffer from addiction. At some point, the year is not known, Grand Maw's bother Bud came to live with them. Grand Maw also had four half sisters, but they always kept their distance from her. They didn't want people to know that they were related to her because they were ashamed of what she had done.

I was told that Grand Maw would walk to town to get morphine, and she would take little Mary with her and that she would put a veil over her head so that no one could see her face. One day they were walking to town, and they passed by a lady's house, and there was a pear tree in her yard next to the road. Grand Maw stopped and picked up a pear off the ground. There were a lot of them that had fallen on the ground, and the lady came to the door and said, "Ann, you put that down and get on down the road." Grand Maw didn't say anything. She put the pear down, and she and Little Mary walked on away. There was rejection and persecution everywhere they went. People would look at them strangely. Some people would poke fun at them. They were talked about on every side.

2
Heartache but There Will Be Help

Time was going by. Little Mary had become school age. Grand Maw did not want her to go to school because she knew that people would talk about her, but she took her to the school, and she talked to the teacher. The teacher looked at Grand Maw and said, "Ann, Mary cannot go to school, and you know why." When little Mary was born, there was a doctor who came to Grand Maw and Grandpa's house and delivered her, and he signed her birth certificate that she was white, but because she had brown skin, little Mary was not accepted in society. She never had the privilege of going to school. This brought a lot of pain on all the family. Things were not getting any better, but God was merciful, and he helped them through his love and grace.

Grand Maw said that she would keep her at home and do the best that she could. Little Mary did not understand, but she did not say anything. She was getting big enough to help do a few things around the house, and when Grandpa would go out in the field to work, she began going with him. He taught her how to plant vegetables in the garden. He also taught her how to work in the hay and to milk cows. She worked every day with him. She said that she enjoyed working in the field, and she loved learning how to do all the things that had to be done, but when Grand Maw would walk to town, she would have to walk with her. Sometimes while on their way, Grand Maw would have to sit down on the ground for a while, and then she would get up, and they would walk on to town to get some morphine. Sometimes while on their way, they would have to walk by the Hollygrove School, and the children there would look at them and pick up rocks and throw at them. When they would get to the drugstore, Grand Maw would have to lie down on the floor for a while, and she would get up and take a dose of the morphine. Then she would sit there or lie back down until she could feel the effect of the drug, and then they would walk back home. All this situation was very sad, but they made it day by day. They were criticized and put down. They were rejected and pushed aside. They were talked about and ostracized, but they made it.

Time went on. In the year 1909, Paul met a lady and got married. Her name was Maud Kell. They moved in a little house that was on the land that Grandpa and Grand Maw owned. It was close to where they lived. In the year 1910 or maybe 1911, Grand Maw's daddy came to live with them. His wife had died. He had been living with his other daughters, but he decided to go and live with Grand Maw and Grandpa. Their house was very small, and with all the people who lived there, it was crowded, but they all tried to help one another the best that they could. They did not have the money to buy everything that they needed. Grandpa was working every day, and Grand Maw was taking everything that she could sell to get the drug. Sometimes she would ask Grandpa if he had a little money, and he would have to tell her no. It is said that when wrong choices are made, it causes a lot of pain and brings so much hurt on innocent people, and that is what Grand Maw did.

Hoping for Better Things

Everyone in the family was hoping and praying that Grand Maw would change and do better and stop taking the morphine. Her problem affected everyone, and there was nothing that they could do to help her. The situation looked and seemed impossible. It took a very long time, but as this story goes on, you will see how God and his love and mercy intervened and brought good out of this, because there is nothing impossible with God.

Time was going by. In the year 1912, Jim met a lady, and they got married. Her name was Maggie Jones. They did not live on Grandpa and Grand Maw's land. They moved farther out, closer to town, but they would come and visit with them often. Maggie did not have a problem with the family situation being like it was, but everyone was still hoping that things would get better.

Grand Maw was still doing what she thought she had to do to get the drug. It is not known why Grand Maw stopped walking to Belfast to get the morphine, but she had begun walking to Lewisburg. It was farther to walk, and it took longer, but she would still go there. In those days, there were two or maybe three drugstores in town. There was one that I was told about. The name of it was Brawles. It is not known for sure which one that Grand Maw went to and got her morphine, but I was told that the man who owned the drugstore began to talk to Grand Maw and to proposition her to let him have relations with little Mary in exchange for the morphine, and Grand Maw was willing to do this. I was never told how long this went on, but I was told that little Mary would say to the man, "Leave me alone." I was not told the man's name.

As little Mary kept maturing, she was never bitter against her mother. She always stood by her and tried to help her in every way that she could, but she was always hoping and praying that her mother would change and get better. One day Grand Maw and Mary decided to go and see Lilly and her family. It was a short distance to where they lived, and they walked to their house. Lilly was cooking dinner, and she was glad to see them. She asked them to eat with them. I was told that she had a real good dinner; and when she got everything prepared and put on the table ready for everyone to sit down and eat, James, her husband, came in the kitchen and went over to the table and picked up everything that Lilly had fixed and took it to the back door and threw it all out in the yard because he didn't want Grand Maw and Mary to eat. It hurt Lilly real bad. Grand Maw and Mary did not say anything. They just got up and went home. James did not like Grand Maw and Mary. He would rather that they stay away and not ever come to see them. James did not treat Lilly good. She went through a lot of pain because James felt the way he did about her family and the way that he treated her.

Paul and his wife, Maud, would come to see Grandpa and Grand Maw often. They didn't have a problem with the family situation. Time was going by. Mary was growing up. Grand Maw was still taking the morphine when she could get it. Things were real bad for all of them. Sometime maybe in the year 1915, Grandpa sold a lot of his land to a man and his wife who lived close to Grandpa and Grand Maw. Their names were JN and Sammy Caughran. They also owned a building that was in front of their house, and they started selling potatoes there. Later in the year 1916, they started a store there, and they sold groceries and clothes and shoes and all kinds of things. They were doing good, and they decided to start a peddling truck, and they would carry groceries to people's houses in town and in the country. They also carried live chickens in a cage on the back of the peddling truck. This was a great help to people.

Grandpa and Grand Maw would walk to the store to get things that they needed. Mary was now about sixteen. She was still helping Grandpa work in the field, and she was doing all that she could to help Grand Maw. She loved her mother very much. As time went by, Mary met a young man. He was a white man. I was not told how she met him. It could have been at the store because he drove the peddling truck for Mr. Caughran for a long time. His name was Ernest Craig. He began going to see Mary, and she fell in love with him. They dated for a long time. He never said anything to her about marriage because he didn't feel the same for Mary as she did for him, but on February 11, 1918, Mary gave birth to a baby girl. She named her Ethel. She had white skin, and she looked like her daddy. She was born at home, and Grand Maw delivered her before the doctor got there, but when he did get there, he signed Ethel's birth certificate that she was white.

Mary loved her baby, and she took real good care of her. Ernest had to go in service while Mary was pregnant with Ethel, and in April 1918, he had to go overseas in World War I. Ethel was two months old, and he stayed until July 1919. Mary waited for him, hoping that everything would work out for the good for them. When he got home, Mary became pregnant again, and she gave birth to another baby girl. She named her Brownie. I was not told the year and month of Brownie's birth, but she died a day or two after she was born.

Mary loved Ernest. He stayed with her for a long time. He had a problem with drinking, and he would leave home a lot and stay until it was real late at night. Mary didn't know where he was, but she would stay up and keep his food warm for him.

When Will the Pain Ease

Mary began working for different people. She would clean their house and wash and iron their clothes. Mr. and Mrs. Caughran was one family that she worked for. She helped take care of their children while they worked in the store. They had two sons. Mary would work most every day for someone. She would walk to work. Sometimes she would take Ethel with her because Grand Maw would be too sick to keep her or she would be going to get morphine. There were times that it would be raining, but Mary would still walk to work. The distance was not very far. But she had a real hard time. The people liked Mary's work. They were well pleased with how she did her work, but they kept their distance from her.

When the year 1920 came, Grandpa was beginning to get sick. His health was getting bad. Lilly was pregnant in that year. She already had five children, and this one would make six for her and James. It is not known how many months that she was with the child, but it was told that Lilly fell and hurt herself. She had lacerations on her face and body, and she died. Mary was working for some people when this happened, and James never went and told Grand Maw and Grandpa and Mary until she was already buried. It hurt Grand Maw and Grandpa and Mary real bad. It was said by the family that James did something to Lilly that caused this to happen, but they never said anything to him about it. This happened on June 29, 1920, and it was not very long after Lilly died that her and James's five children had to go to an orphans' home. They stayed there until they became adults, and on September 1 of the same year, Grandpa died.

Everything began to get real bad. All the load was on Mary's back, but she kept on working and doing all that she could to help her family. There were times when Mary would be working and the people would be having dinner, and Mary would not ask for anything, but they would give her a piece of bread. When the holidays would come at Christmastime, they would give her a stick of peppermint candy. She said that she would eat just a little at one time to make it last for a while.

Time was going by. Grand Maw was still on the morphine, but she seemed to be getting a little better. Money was hard to get when the year 1924 came. Ethel was school age. Mary took her to the school and talked to the teacher, but she said that they could not accept her. Even though Ethel had white skin, it did not matter. It was because her mother, Mary, had brown skin. It was a sad situation, and Ethel felt real sad about it. She was denied the privilege of going to school.

Grand Maw taught Mary how to write her name, and she taught Ethel to spell and to write a lot of things, but Ethel's daddy, Ernest, would help her with her reading. He taught her a lot, and she enjoyed learning. Ernest lived with them for a long time, and then he decided to leave and go live with some other people, but he would come by to see Ethel a lot of times. Mary missed him after he left, but she never complained. Ethel was always glad and happy when he would come to see her. Sometimes when there would come a day that Mary didn't have to work or maybe she would get through early and if the day was pretty and clear, they would walk to town, and they would have to pass by the little one-room schoolhouse where the children in the neighborhood went and where Ethel would have gone if she had been accepted. She felt sad, and sometimes she would cry, but she didn't say anything. There were times that tears were shed by Grand Maw, Mary, and Ethel; but there was nothing that they could do about the situation being like it was.

Time went on, and in the year 1926, Grand Maw's daddy, George Craig, died. This now left just Grand Maw, Mary, and Ethel. Grand Maw's brother Bud went to live with some other people. It is not known who the people were. Everything was still so hard for them. They could not keep working the little farm like they should because Mary could not work on the farm and work for other people too, but she tried so hard to do all that she could. Grand Maw would help do what she could. Her health was getting real bad, but she was not taking as much morphine as she had been. Ethel was growing up. She would help them do some things. Sometimes she would feed the chickens and go with Mary and Grand Maw to milk the cows. Grand Maw taught Mary how to sew, and when she could get some flour sacks or feed sacks, she would make Ethel a dress or some panties. At that time, flour and feed for the cows and horses came in sacks that were cloth, and they had real pretty flowers on them.

As time went by, they were still being rejected and talked about. At some point, Mary asked Grand Maw, "Why am I like I am?" Grand Maw told her that when she was pregnant with her, a colored man scared her, and that marked her, and that was why she was like that. Mary didn't ask or say anything else, but deep inside, she knew that was not the way it was. Grand Maw's health was getting worse, and she finally gave up the morphine. She didn't take any more. She changed her life, and she said to Mary, "One day I once was blind, but now I can see."

Mary said that she cried a lot of tears over her mother, and she prayed a lot of prayers. On January 8, 1929, Grand Maw died. She was sixty years old. Mary and Ethel were left alone. Ethel was eleven years old. They kept living at the same place for a long time. Mary continued to work for Mr. Caughran and also for other people. Ethel would walk with her to work and help her all that she could. Mary missed her mother very much, but she knew that life had to go on.

In the year 1935 or maybe 1936, Mary had to sell the little farm. Mr. Caughran bought the house and the land. She had to sell the cows and the other animals that they had, and they moved to another house. It was maybe about three miles from where they lived. The house belonged to Mr. Marvin Jones. They lived there for a long time. Mary would wash and iron for a lot of people. Some of them would bring their clothes to her house, and when she would get them ready, they would come back and pick them up.

Ethel was about eighteen at this time. There was a young man whom she got to know. It is not known how she met him, but he showed interest in her. He was a white man and he came to see her for a few times, and then he had to go in service. He was gone for a long time. He would write to her often. Then there was another young man whom she got to know. He was also a white man, and he came and dated her for a while, and then he had to go in service and was gone for a very long time.

Ethel's daddy, Ernest, didn't come to see her as often as he did. He met another woman, and he married her, and they lived close to town. Her name was Maggy Sue. When Ethel met her, they got along together real well and loved each other. It was always a very happy time for Ethel when her daddy would come by to see her. She loved him very much.

3
Struggling with the Disappointment

Times were very hard for Mary and Ethel. Mary worked every day that she could for someone. She washed and ironed and cleaned when she would go to Mr. Caughran's house. They had a washhouse at the back of their house, and Mary would go in there and wash their clothes on a rubboard in a washtub, and then she would take those clothes and put them in a wash kettle. She would build a fire around that old kettle, and she would boil the clothes for a while, and then she would take them out and put them in another tub for a second rinse. In the second rinse, she would look in a little box that she kept sitting on a shelf, and what was in the little box was blueing. The box had a lot of little balls, and Mary would get three of those little balls and tie them up in a little rag, and then she would swish them around in that rinse. They would make the water blue, but when she would rinse the white clothes in the water, they would be much whiter. She would then take them and hang them on the line to dry, and then she would go back another day and iron the clothes.

There was also a storm cellar at the back of the house, and sometimes when it was raining or real cold, Mary would go down in the cellar and take the washtubs down there and wash. Sometimes Ethel would go with her and help her, but most of the time, Ethel would stay home and clean the house and cook. She learned to be a good cook. She would have dinner ready when Mary would get home.

Time went on, and in the year 1939 or maybe 1940, Mary began washing for a family who lived in Belfast. They would bring their clothes to her house and come back and pick them up. It was a man and his wife. Their names were Edd and Clair Eakes. Clair worked in town, but I was told that she was sick a lot, and sometimes she could not work. There had been a time that she was in the yard, and it began to storm. Lightning came down and struck her, and she got better but was never the same.

Edd was a blacksmith, and he was also a deputy sheriff for a short time. One day when he brought their clothes to Mary and Ethel's house, he saw Ethel and began talking with her. He was very attracted to her, and soon they began seeing each other. He was a white man, and he was a lot older than Ethel. This went on for a long time, and in the year 1941, Ethel became pregnant. In April 1942, she gave birth to a baby girl. She was born at home, and Ethel named her Mary Ann, and that is me. A doctor came to the house and delivered me. His name was Dr. Paul Foster. I have white skin, but my birth certificate stated that my mother was Negro. My mother never said anything to the doctor about changing the birth certificate.

Making It Through

Things began to be harder for my mother and grandmother. They had to take care of me. They worked all they could, and they loved me and took real good care of me. Time went by, and in the year 1944 or 1945, Mr. Caughran, the man whom my grandmother was still working for, owned a house about three or maybe four miles from where his store was. It had about twelve acres of land that went with it. He wanted to sell it to my grandmother, and they sat down one day and talked about it. Mr. Caughran worked everything out for her to make payments.

It was a real old house, and it was about a half mile up a real rocky lane from the main road. I was too little to remember when they moved there. There was no water in the house, but there was a well in the backyard, and they had to draw water for drinking and for washing clothes. The water was sulfur, and sometimes it would turn almost black. There was a fireplace in two of the rooms. It was real hard in the wintertime. My grandmother would go out in the woods and cut wood to make a fire in those fireplaces to keep us warm.

My daddy, Edd, would come and see us often. He would still bring their clothes for grandmother to wash and iron. He would help cut some wood and bring it to the house. Sometimes he also would give Mother a little money to help with things for me. Grandmother got us some chickens, and the hens would lay eggs, and that was a help. It was not ever known if Miss Clair, Daddy's wife, ever knew about me. There was a lot of talk about her sickness, and in the year 1947, she committed suicide. She took an overdose of something. No one knew what it was, and it was not very long after that happened that Mother and Daddy got married. Then people began talking. They would say that Edd married a black woman. There was always talk from people.

Daddy had a wonderful talent working with wood. He had a trailer that he built, and he put wheels on it, and he could pull it behind a car. He and Clair lived in it, and when he and Mother got married, he pulled it to our house. He connected it to our house. Daddy continued to work in the blacksmith business, and he also did a lot of work at home. He would plant and work a garden and raise a lot of our food. In the evening, when Grandmother would get home from work, she would go out in the garden and help Daddy, and Mother would help also when she was not busy in the house. There was a lot to do.

More Talk and Criticism

A short time after Mother and Daddy had got married, one day a man came to our house. He was a constable. He talked with Mother. Daddy was not at home. He was working for someone. The man told Mother and Grandmother that all of them would have to go to the courthouse. He told them what day for them to be there, and when that day came, Mother and Daddy and Grandmother went to the courthouse. They took me with them. I was five years old, and I can't remember everything, but I can remember when we all went in one of the rooms where the judge was. His name was Judge Holly. He talked with Daddy and Mother, and it was about Daddy marrying a black woman. I cannot remember what all that was said, but I do still remember that the judge looked at my grandmother and pointed his finger at her and said, "Now you, you are colored."

My grandmother looked at him and said with a soft voice, "I am what I am." I don't remember him saying anything else to her. He talked a little more with Daddy and Mother, and then he told them that they could go. Daddy was talked about and rejected just like the rest of us was. Almost every Saturday, we would go to town. Daddy would go to the hardware store and get horseshoes and nails to shoe horses for people. He was real good at his job as a blacksmith. He went to a lot of people's houses to shoe their horses. They liked his work, but they kept their distance from him.

There was also a doctor in town, and he would see people when they were sick. If they didn't have the money to pay him, then he would charge it for them until later when they did have it. We all would go and see him when we needed to. He was a very good doctor.

There was a drugstore on the square in town. They would also charge medicine for people who did not have the money at the time, and they could go later and pay. There were times that Mother and Daddy and Grandmother would have to charge their medicine, but Grandmother would always go back and pay them. The drugstore had a soda fountain, and I always enjoyed going there. I was never turned away. Sometimes Mother or Grandmother would give me a nickel or maybe a dime, and I would walk up to the counter and sit down on one of the stools. The lady who worked there would ask me what I wanted, and I would get a drink or ice cream. That was a real pleasure to me to get to do that. Nobody talked to me, but that was part of the rejection that we all went through.

I remember one day we were in town, and there was a public restroom that was close to the square, but it was for white people only. I told Mother that I had to use the restroom, and she said to me, "I will take you to the restroom, but I don't know if the lady there will let you use it or not." So we went in, and the lady met us. Mother asked her if I could use the restroom, and the lady said no, that I could not. Mother held my hand, and we walked out. Mother did not say anything, but it hurt her feelings, and we went home.

Daddy and Mother and Grandmother would go to the store and buy their groceries Mr. Caughran would charge people's groceries for them. He would write every item down on paper and put their name on it and keep it until they came back to pay. I was always happy when we would go to the store. Grandmother would buy me some candy and an RC Cola.

Daddy's health began to get bad, and he could not work a lot. He had ulcers in his stomach. He suffered a lot with that, but he worked as much as he could. Through all the rejections and being talked about and put down, Grandmother and Mother never held any bitterness against anyone. Grandmother held her head up and showed love because she knew that God was there, and he would always take care of her and her family.

Time was going by, and I became school age. Daddy said that he wanted to do whatever he could to get me in school. I mentioned earlier in this story that my birth certificate stated that my mother was Negro, and also I was given Mother's maiden name because Mother and Daddy were not married at the time I was born. Daddy wanted to have that changed, so they went to a lawyer in town. He was also a judge. They talked to him about changing my name to Daddy's name, and the lawyer agreed. He fixed all the paperwork and got that done, and Daddy asked him about changing the birth certificate to white instead of Negro. The lawyer looked at Daddy and said, "You can change a name, but you cannot change a color." He said he would not do it.

Mother and Daddy were hurt bad because he refused, and they went and talked to another lawyer and told him all about the situation. He agreed to change my birth certificate, and he began working on it. When he got the paperwork fixed, he had to send it to the courthouse to be notarized, and the first lawyer who had refused to change it called the courthouse and told the notary that under no circumstances should the paper be notarized. So there was nothing that Mother and Daddy could do. They talked to a lot of people, hoping that something could be done, but there was nothing. One day

Mother and Daddy were at Mr. Caughran's store, and the school bus driver who drove in that community was there, and Mother overheard him say, "If Edd and Ethel have Mary Ann at the bus stop, I will not pick her up." I felt real sad about it all. I was hoping so much that I would get to go to school.

Making it by Grace

We all had to face being pushed aside, but we held our heads up, and by God's amazing grace, we made it. We were disappointed, and we were hurt, but we had to accept what was. God gave us strength to make it. Mother and Daddy bought me first-grade books to read at home. Mother helped me, and I learned to read. I had a desire to learn. I also loved to sing. I would listen to the old radio that we had. It was a battery radio, and when Saturday night would come, I would listen to the *Grand Ole Opry*, and I learned a lot of the songs that the *Opry* people sang. I spent a lot of time singing.

Daddy bought me a bicycle. He put me a training wheel on one side of it to learn to ride. Our house did not have electricity. Grandmother would light the old kerosene lamps, and that was all the light that we had. Daddy decided that he would wire our house. He didn't have the money to pay someone else to wire it, so he began working on it. He got it wired, and he did a good job, but when he had to talk with the electric company, they were going to have to put an electric pole in a field that belonged to a family who lived on the main road. That family did not want the pole put there on their land. Mother and Daddy and Grandmother were real discouraged about it, but after a period, that family agreed to let them put the electric pole there, and we got electricity in our house. All of us were so happy. We felt like that was the best thing that ever happened to us. Daddy bought some big light bulbs, and they shone so bright. Grandmother soon bought us an electric stove, and that was a blessing because she didn't have to build a fire every morning in the old woodstove to cook breakfast.

There was an old barn that was close to our house. Sometimes I would go down there and go in one of the stables and sing. I spent a lot of my time singing, but I also would read my books over and over, and Mother would help me. Grandmother and Mother and Daddy bought three or maybe four cows, and they would milk those cows and sell the milk. I remember they would put the milk in a milk can, and Daddy would take it to the end of the lane to the main road for the milk truck to pick up. Daddy built himself a slide to put the milk can on. He had a mule, and he would hook him up to that old slide, and he would pull the can to the road. Sometimes I would get on that slide and sit down and ride with him.

Mother and Daddy would still talk to different people, hoping that someone could help to get me in school, but there was no way. I remember Mother and Daddy and Grandmother heard from some source about a fortune-teller who lived in another town, and they went a few times and talked to him. One day a car came up the old rocky lane to our house, and it was the fortune-teller and his wife. They sat in their car and talked with Mother and Daddy about me. They wanted Mother and Daddy to let me go and live with them, and they would get me in school in their town. The town they lived in was about twenty-five miles from where we lived. Mother and Daddy gave it some thought, but I did not want to go live with them, and Mother and Daddy never insisted for me to go. It probably would not have helped because of the birth certificate, so after a period, they accepted that I would not get to go to school.

I kept busy. I would help Grandmother when she would do her work. I would go with her often when she would go to Mr. Caughran's house to work. She would go on Monday and wash their clothes, and then she would go back on Thursday and iron. Daddy would still go shoe horses for people when he was able, and sometimes I would go with him. There were two other families who lived just a little ways from Mr. Caughran's store: Mr. and Mrs. Woodard and Mr. and Mrs. Batten. Grandmother would wash for the Woodards, and she would clean the house for the Battens. I would go with her to clean, and she would give me a dollar when she got paid.

Grandmother would go out to the chicken house and feed the chickens, and I would be there with her, and she would let me help her. I really enjoyed throwing down corn for those chickens. I learned to do a lot of things around the house. Mother began teaching me how to cook, and I would try. I remember how I would stand beside her and watch her when she would bake a cake or a pie. It was a joy to me to learn.

There was a big oak tree that was close to our house, and sometimes I would go out and play around that tree, and I would wish for someone to play with. I mentioned earlier in this story about the family who took a while to decide to let the light pole be put on their land so we could have electricity. I remember one day it was a beautiful sunny day. I was walking with Grandmother down the old rocky lane to the main road, and we were about to walk by their house. They had about five children, and some of the children and their mother were out in the yard. Grandmother stopped and talked to them, and one of the girls talked to me, and she asked me to come out and play with them sometime. It made me so happy that I would have someone to play with, so when we went home, I asked Mother if I could go and play with them. She did not give me an answer right then, but later she said I could go. I began going sometimes to play with them. They were very nice to me, and I enjoyed being with them. I asked them one day while I was there to come to my house and play, but they never did.

One day when I was there, I stayed maybe an hour with the girls, and their mother came to me and gave me a little note and said, "Mary Ann, give this to your mother." I took the note and left to go home, and as I walked up that rocky lane, I sat down on a big rock, and I looked at the note. I tried to read it, but I could not make it all clear, so when I got home, I gave it to Mother. She read it, and it said, "Ethel, keep Mary Ann at home. I am sick and don't feel like being bothered with children." Mother never said anything. She just told me that I could not go back, and I never went back anymore. It hurt me, but I didn't say anything. I tried to entertain myself. Sometimes I would think about school, and I would be sad because I didn't get to go. I missed out on a lot like going the first day of school and meeting the teacher and seeing all the rows of desks and chairs and the blackboard and getting to know the children. But I was making it, and everything was going to be all right.

I was real close to Grandmother. Just about everywhere that she went, I went with her. When she would go and wash clothes, I would try to help her. I would rub a few things on the old rubboard, and then my hands would get tired, and I would stop. She would start rubbing those clothes.

There was a lady who was a relative of Mr. Caughran, and she moved in with him and his son. She worked in town, but she would cook a lot of their food, and she would help with the cleaning. Her name was Miss Sara. Grandmother would wash her clothes also. When she washed for the others, I mentioned earlier about the flour sacks. A lot of the ladies saved them because once a month when a lady's cycle would come around, they used those flour sacks because some of them did not have the money to buy pads. Mother would put her sacks in a bucket of water and wash them and rinse them. I was told that a lot of ladies did the same. Grandmother would wash all the clothes that this family had that needed to be washed, and then she would take those flour sacks that Miss Sara used and rub them on the rubboard until they were clean. When she would go back to iron their clothes, she would iron those sacks and fold them neatly for her to use again.

There Will Be Help for a Brighter Day

Mother always taught me to believe in God. I remember when she would sit in the old rocking chair, and I would sit in her lap, and she would rock me and tell me about Jesus, that he loved me and that he could do all things. Time was going by. When Christmas would come, I always loved that time of the year. Daddy would go down in the woods and cut down a tree and bring it to the house, and he would put it up in front of the window. Grandmother and Mother would put Christmas balls on it and a few more decorations that we had. Grandmother would put a little flour in a cup and pour a little water in it and mix it up, and it would be like a paste. She would take a spoon and put a little of that paste on the tree, and it would look like it had snow on it. It would be so pretty when they would get through with it.

Mother would bake a coconut cake, and Grandmother would bake a pineapple cake and put egg white icing on it. Then she would take small pieces of pineapple and put them all on top and on the sides of the cake. Mother and Daddy always put me a gift under the tree. Sometimes it would be a new pair of shoes or some kind of toy. Things were hard sometimes, but we continued to make it through with God's help.

As time went on, there was a man and his wife who lived on the main road. They didn't have any children. They were very good people. They milked cows. Their names were Mr. and Mrs. Davis. One day Mr. Davis came and talked to Grandmother about milking for him in the afternoon, and she told him that she would take the job. I started going with her. She taught me how to milk those cows. They did not have milkers. She had to milk them by hand. When we would get through, we would walk home. Grandmother would be tired, and she would sit down and rest for a little while, and then she would get up and begin other chores at the house.

Grandmother and Mother and Daddy stayed strong through everything that we had been through and still were going through, but they took courage and believed and trusted in God to take us through and to always make a way and to supply all our needs, and he did. They did the best that they could and left the rest in God's hands because he knew what to do when they didn't.

4

Something Good Was About to Happen

There was a family who lived about two or maybe three miles from us. Mother and Daddy and Grandmother knew them, and the lady was attending a small church in town. One beautiful sunny day, they came to our house to visit, and she asked Mother if I could go to church with her, and Mother said that I could. I was about eleven years old. I was so glad that this lady asked for me to go to church. It thrilled my heart so much. Her name was Annie May, and one Sunday night, I went to church with her. I remember so well I enjoyed it so much. It was the best thing that ever happened to me. When the service started, I sat there and listened to the people sing, and then I listened to the pastor preach, and when he got through preaching, he asked everyone who would to come down for prayer for whatever they needed and anyone who wanted to give their heart to the Lord. There were a few people who got up and went down, and I got up also and went down, and I kneeled down at the altar. I gave my heart to Jesus, and I let him come into my heart and life. I was so happy. The people in the church accepted me, and they treated me good.

I began going every Sunday. The church had a bus, and they would pick up people and bring them to church. Daddy would take me to Annie May's house, and I would wait with her for the bus to pick us up. I did not want to miss church. After a period, the church bus broke down, and some of the people at church would go and pick up the ones who needed a way there. There was a man and his wife. They were both ministers. They lived in Shelbyville, Tennessee. They had three children, and they would come by the old lane and pick me up every Sunday morning. I would walk down the lane to the road to meet them. They would bring another young lady with them. She lived close to where they lived. She was near my age, and she and I became good friends. I told her that I did not get to go to school, and she wanted to help me. Sometimes she would bring her schoolbooks to church, and she would teach me about different things from them before service would start.

Having Good Times

I was more happy than I had ever been. This young lady's name was Jannie Ruth. Sometimes she would go home with me after church and stay until church that night, and sometimes I would ask Mother if I could go home with her and spend the evening with her. Mother would say that I could. We had real good times together. When we were in church, we would go in Sunday school. I really loved that I learned so much. Our Sunday school teacher was Sister Annie Lee, and she taught us about Jesus and how we had to believe and trust in him. She would tell us that Jesus had all power and that he could do anything.

The pastor was Brother Carrol; and his wife, Sister Ceppel, would sing and play the guitar. Our Sunday school teacher, Sister Annie, would also sing and play the guitar. I loved to hear them sing. They began asking me to sing, and I was real nervous, but I soon got better. Mother had a real old guitar, and she had learned about three chords on it, and she taught me. I had a desire to learn, and I would watch Sister Annie Lee when she would play and sing, and I learned a little more how to play.

I remember the first song that I sang in church. It was an old song that Martha Carson sang, "Lazarus Lazarus." Soon I got baptized. There were two other ladies who got baptized at the same time that I did. It was on Sunday evening after church. Brother Carrol, our pastor, took us to a creek; and we went in the water. It was a cloudy day and kinda cold, but no one got sick. I was so happy. Mother and Grandmother were real happy for me, but Daddy's health was getting worse. His kidneys were failing. He was in a lot of pain. He could not work anymore. Things were real bad. Money was short. Grandmother was doing all she could to keep the bills paid.

I remember there was one time that Daddy had to go to the hospital, and the doctors had to put a tube in his stomach, and his kidneys acted through the tube. A lot of nights he would not sleep because his pain was so bad. I mentioned earlier in this story that Daddy was a lot older than Mother. He had two sons by his first wife. Her name was Maggy. The eldest son's name was Newman, and the other one's name was JD. Newman lived in Texas and JD in Louisiana. They would come to see Daddy sometimes.

JD would come to see us more than Newman did. He always had a new car, and he would drive it up the old rocky lane. He did not have a problem with our family situation. He was married at that time to a very rich woman, and they owned five drive-in restaurants around Louisiana. He would help Daddy with things that he needed like pants and shirts, and if I needed a coat or a dress, he would buy them for me. This was a great help for us because we were having a hard time. Mother and Daddy decided to go and ask for some help from the welfare, and they did give them help for Daddy and me.

I was still excited and happy about going to church. I would sing and try real hard to read my Bible. JD knew that I sing, and he came up to see us one day. He told me that he wanted to take me to Nashville. He was willing to pay as much as it would cost for me to get a record cut, but I told him that I didn't want to. I wanted to keep singing at church. I was learning so much at church. Everyone there was so good to me. They showed love and kindness, and they were glad that I was there, and I had a great desire to be there. Grandmother would encourage me in every way that she could about church.

Daddy decided one Sunday that he would go with me, and everyone welcomed him and treated him good. Some of the people at church knew about our family circumstances, but they never said anything to me about it. They never went and asked Mother and

Grandmother to come to church, but all of them were kind to me. Sometimes when it would be real cold, Daddy would drive me down the old lane to meet Brother and Sister Singleton. They would always come by and pick me up.

The car that Daddy had was real old, but he wanted me to learn to drive, and he began to teach me. I tried real hard, and it didn't take me very long to learn. Grandmother began to teach me how to sew, and I loved learning. Grandmother would make me a dress sometimes, and I was always proud of that dress. She would sew a lot just with a needle and thread with her hands, but she had an old pedal sewing machine, and she would use it sometimes. Grandmother had a determination and a great drive within her, so strong that she would climb every mountain life presented, and she would walk through every valley with patience. She held her head up because she knew that God was walking by her side. The Bible says, "If God be for you, who can be against you?" I loved spending time with her and learning how to do a lot of things.

Mother would also help me in every way she could. I love to cook and bake today, and Mother taught me. I have a lot of wonderful memories of Mother and Grandmother and all the good times that we had together. As I was growing up, I remember a lot of times when it would be real cold at night when I would go to bed. Grandmother would get a sweater or whatever she could find, and she would hold it by the fire in the old fireplace until it would get warm, and then she would bring it to where I was lying and wrap it around my feet to keep me warm.

Growing Up Too Quick

Time was still going by, and I was thirteen. I was still enjoying going to church. I would never miss going unless I was sick. Annie May, the lady who started taking me to church, had a stepson; and he wanted to date me. He was twenty-one, but Mother and Daddy agreed, and we began dating. He would come to the house to see me. This was maybe in October or November of 1955, and in February of 1956, we got married. I was so young. We had to go to

Mississippi. Daddy went with us, and he signed for me. The son of Mr. Caughran, the man whom grandmother still worked for, who lived in town drove us to Mississippi. It was a long day.

We lived in the small trailer that Daddy had built and connected it to the house. My husband's name was Willie, and he worked in town at a horse barn. He would feed the horses and help train them, and sometimes he would have to take a horse to another town. There were a few times that I would go with him. Things were going good, and in April 1957, I gave birth to a baby girl. We named her Sharon. I was real sick almost the whole time of my pregnancy. I went to our family doctor. He treated me good.

At the end of my nine months, I began having real hard pains, and Willie took me to the hospital. Mother went with us. When we got there, one of the nurses took me up to the third floor. That floor was smaller than the first and second floors, and there they put the black people. There was a black lady in the next room from me. She had just had a baby. The nurse brought things that were needed up in my room. I was to have my baby in my room, but I stayed in labor from about eleven thirty that day until the next morning. They called the doctor, and he came to the hospital, and he had them to bring me down to the delivery room.

My daughter was born about 4:30 a.m., and the nurse returned me to my room. They brought my baby in a hospital bassinet in my room. She never stayed in the nursery with the other babies. When I went home, Mother and Grandmother helped me all they could. There was so much that I had to learn. I was so glad when I could take her to church with me. I turned fifteen a week after Sharon was born.

Daddy was getting a lot worse. His kidneys were failing, and he was in so much pain. One day he was sitting in a chair, and Mother picked up Sharon from the bed and laid her in his lap. He held her for just a few minutes. He got so bad that he could not walk, and he could not eat, and on June 18 of that same year, Daddy died. Mother had his funeral at home. It was a very sad time for all of us. There was a cemetery not very far from where we lived, maybe three or four miles, and Daddy had told Mother that he wanted to be buried there. Mother located the people who were over the cemetery, and they would not let her bury him there. They said that no one had been buried there in a long time. Mother didn't say anything. It hurt her feelings. She had Daddy buried where his mother was buried, and it was about fifteen miles from where we lived. We all had a hard time, but we made it by God's help.

In March of the next year, 1958, I gave birth to another baby girl; and we named her Pamela Sue. There was an eleven-month difference between Sharon and Sue. Most everyone called her Sue. There were a few people who called her Pam. I had two babies. There was another doctor in town whom I began seeing while I was pregnant with Sue, and he delivered her. He treated me good. I was in the room with another lady who had a baby. She was a white lady. When I got home, I had a hard time with two babies in diapers and on bottles, but Mother and Grandmother helped me. I took my babies to church.

When Sharon was born, I received her birth certificate, and it said, "Mother: Colored." When Sue was born, I received her birth certificate, and it said, "Mother: Negro." We began to wonder if it would be the same when they became school age, but all I could do was pray and trust God to work it out. I began to sew and to make a lot of their clothes. Grandmother would help me when they became one and two years old. I wanted to get a job. Extra money would help so much.

There was a small restaurant in town, and I went there and asked about a job. The lady who was the owner talked to me, and she told me that she would hire me to work. I was so excited. She told me to come on a certain day, and when I went back, she told me that she could not let me work. I did not understand at first, but then I learned that she was told about my family situation. It hurt me real bad, but there was nothing that I could do about it. I could not get a job anywhere in town because things were that way. I became real discouraged. I began to lose my desire to go to church. Soon I quit going and stayed home. I didn't seem to realize that God was my help through everything. The Bible says that he is a present help in times of trouble.

Time was going by, and one day my brother came to see us. I mentioned earlier in the story JD, the one who was married to the lady who had a lot of money. At this time, he had remarried, and he and his wife had moved to Tennessee in a small town called Fayetteville. They had opened a restaurant, and they asked if Willie and I would be willing to move there and go to work with them. Willie did not want to move there, but I did, so he agreed. We made the decision to move. I began working in the restaurant, and I learned so much. Willie worked the gas pumps out front. We lived with JD and his wife, Marion, for a while; and I went to the government housing projects. I filled out an application for an apartment, and it was not very long until they gave us one. I was happy about it. This was the first time that we lived in a house that had a bathroom inside and a sink with running water in the kitchen. I had a bathtub that I could get in and sit down and take a bath.

Some Things Began to Change

Shortly before we got the apartment, my brother JD and Marion had to close the restaurant, and I had to have a job. There was a restaurant down the road, and I asked about a job there, and they hired me. We were having a hard time. Willie needed a job also. I worked at night, and he kept the children, but he did not like living there. It was not very long until he moved back to Lewisburg. He lived with Mother and Grandmother for a while, but I stayed and worked. I was doing good on my job.

We needed furniture. All that we had were some odds and ends that Mother gave me. I went to a furniture store in Lewisburg, and I asked about getting some things that I needed on credit and pay so much a month, and the owner of the store told me that I could. I bought a living room suit and a dining table and chairs. They were so pretty. I had never had anything that nice before. I worked six nights a week.

When Willie moved, Mother began keeping my children. It was very hard to find someone to keep them all night, and it was also hard for me to sleep in the daytime and watch them too, so

Mother watched them most of the time. On my day off, I would go to Mother's house and spend the day and be with them. There was a bus station in Fayetteville, and I would go and ride the bus to Lewisburg. I did not have a car. I was having a hard time paying my rent and also my furniture. Mother and Grandmother helped me all that they could. The Lord always supplied all my needs.

After a period, Willie moved to Alabama and went to work with horses. That's the kind of work that he liked to do, but he would still come and see the children. I was enjoying working at the restaurant. There was more to have to learn there than there was at my brother's restaurant. I learned how to work the cash register and to write out the menus. Working there was an experience for me. I also had to learn how to cook on the grill, but it didn't take me long to learn. I was still not going to church, but I never forgot that Jesus was my present help. He took care of me and extended his mercy and his wonderful, amazing grace.

5

Getting to Know New Friends

At my work, there was a young lady who also worked there. Her name was Nadine, and she and I began spending time together, and we became very good friends. I shared with her about my family situation. She accepted it fine. Sometimes when we could be off from work, we would go to the theater and watch a movie. I got to know her parents. They were very nice and sweet people. They loved my children. I would go and visit with her, and she would come to my house and visit with me, and soon she moved in with me. We shared the apartment for a long time. We would split the rent and utilities together, and then she decided to move back with her parents, but we still stayed friends.

After a period, I filed for a divorce from Willie. He never wanted to come back. The people whom I worked for were very nice. They were real good to me. I had to eat at the restaurant. I didn't have the money to buy food at home, and they never said anything. I got to know a lot of people while working there.

Time was going by. I was having a real hard time. I loved my job, but I became discouraged. I was facing some difficult situations, and I began to pray. I had been taught that prayer changes things. Even though I was not in church and I was not living my life for God like I should, I still knew that God was my answer no matter what the situation was, so I would ask him to help me, and he always met my needs.

There was a sewing factory in town, and my friend Nadine had gone there and got a job. I decided that I would change jobs, and it was possible that I might make more money there, so I went and asked for a job. I had to take a test for speed, and I failed it, and that meant that I didn't get the job. I became more discouraged, and after maybe a week, I decided to go back and try to talk to the boss of the plant. I did get to see and talk with him. I told him that I failed the speed test, but I needed to work. He hired me. I worked for a short time, and I learned and did very good, but I did not like that kind of work as well as I did the restaurant. I did get some experience at another kind of work. I went back to work in the restaurant.

Time was going by. I was still having a lot of problems paying my bills and getting things for my children that they needed. I went into a state of depression, and one day I talked to Mother, and she told me about a minister who was coming to Fayetteville every Sunday afternoon. He was having cottage prayer meetings in some people's houses in the projects not far from where I lived. I knew this minister. It was Brother Harry Shepard. His wife, Sister Annie Lee, was my Sunday school teacher when I began going to church in Lewisburg. I immediately felt in my heart that I needed to go.

When Sunday came, I went, and God began to deal with my heart to rededicate my life back to him, and I did. I looked forward to being in service every Sunday. They would have service in one family's house one Sunday, and the next Sunday it would be in another family's house. I got to know new people. I began singing again, and I loved to sing. Mother had started taking the children to church when they were not with me. They loved to go to church. It was the same little church that I went to when I was a young girl. Mother and the children were accepted there. Everyone treated them good. When the children were with me, I took them to church to the family's house where they were having service.

A Change Began to Take Place

I had changed jobs again. I worked at another restaurant for a while. I had learned, and I got a lot of experience, and I didn't have any problem at all getting a job in a restaurant. They never asked me about my education. One Sunday when I went to church service, there was a young man there. I learned later that he had recently gone through a divorce. He began coming to service every Sunday. We got to know each other, and we began seeing each other. His name was Lee. He had one daughter. Her name was Regina.

I was very concerned about my children. When they were ready to start school, things had changed a lot, but because their birth certificates were like mine, I didn't know if they would be accepted. They stayed with Mother so much while I worked, so she went and signed them up for school, and there was no problem with them going. I was so glad that they were getting to go to school.

Mother had met someone and got married. He was from a small town called Shelbyville, Tennessee. My family had known him and his family for a long time. He was a white man, and he was very good to Mother and Grandmother and to all of us. It did not make any difference to him about our family situation. My children loved him, and he helped them so much.

There was still a lot of rejection that my family went through. I decided to go back to the sewing factory and see if they would hire me back, and they did. The hours were much better for me there.

Time was going by. The pastor who was having church services in the people's houses had stopped coming to Fayetteville. Lee and I were still seeing each other, and sometimes we would go to church out in the country. A little over three years went by, and Lee and I decided to get married. I continued to work at the sewing factory. After about a year, we were living in an apartment.

One day Mother called me and told me that they had a new pastor. It was a lady, and she and her family were from Nashville, Tennessee. They were so happy with her being there. Her name was Sister Gladys Sanders. Mother told me what a wonderful minister she was, and she wanted us to meet her. When Sister Gladys got to know Mother and the children, she also learned about our family's situation, and she went to their house to visit Grandmother. She asked her to come to church, and she decided to go. Mother called me and told me about it, and I was so happy. Sister Gladys was the only one who had ever asked Grandmother to come to church.

A few months went by, and the Lord opened a door for Lee to get a real good job in Lewisburg, and he took it. There was also a sewing factory there in town, and I went there and asked for a job, and I was hired. We moved to Lewisburg. I was so happy to be close to my family and to be able to go to church with them. My children could be with us more. I got to know new people at work. Most people there didn't know me, and they didn't know about my family situation. If there was anyone there who did know anything about it, they didn't say anything. I was treated right there. No one ever asked me about my education.

My two girls, Sharon and Sue, and Regina, Lee's daughter, got to know one another; and they loved one another. They loved to spend time together and play together, but Sharon and Sue began to have problems at school. Some of the children who went to school with them knew about our family situation, and they would talk about them. Some would say hard and hurtful things to them. They rode the school bus, and sometimes it would get bad. When the bus would get to the road where they got off, Grandmother would walk down that old rocky lane to meet them, and the kids on the bus would see her, and they would look at Sharon and Sue and call her bad names. Sometimes they would have a fight on the bus, but there was a little girl who became a very good friend to Sue. The little girl was crippled, and it did not matter to her about our family situation. She loved Sue, and Sue loved her. They spent a lot of time together. There was another young girl whom Sue and Sharon became good friends with.

We began going to church. I was so happy to be in church and to have my family there. Some of the church people welcomed Grandmother, but there were some who were not pleased. Sister Gladys told me that the first Sunday that Grandmother came to church, when she walked in the door, she said to Sister Gladys, "Where do you want me to sit?" Sister Gladys said she told her, "You sit anywhere that you want to sit."

Grandmother gave her heart and life to God, and she was baptized. That was the happiest time in her life. Mother gave her heart and life to God, and she and the children were also baptized.

Happiness and Joy

We all stayed faithful. Grandmother was so full of joy. I made a commitment to God like never before to serve him. God had worked a miracle for my family and me. He gave us favor, and he took a bad situation and brought something good out of it. The Bible says, "Is anything too hard for the Lord?" (Gen. 18:14). There were times that Sister Gladys would come down to the church on a weekday and pray and fast, and some of the ladies would meet there with her. I would be working, but when I got a lunch break, I would go to the church and pray with them.

As time went by, I began to feel God speaking to my heart that he had something for me to do. I did not understand what it was when it first began, but day after day, I could feel his spirit dealing with my heart. He would bring different scriptures to my mind, and then one night I had a dream. I dreamed I saw some little kittens, and they were hungry and needed milk, and their mother was not there. I knew in my spirit that the dream had a meaning. I prayed so many prayers, and then some scriptures came in my mind, and the Lord gave me a message.

I went to my pastor, Sister Gladys, and I talked to her about this, and she told me that God was calling me into the ministry to preach his word. I was already feeling in my spirit that was what the Lord wanted me to do, but I felt like I could not do that, but Sister Gladys encouraged me to do what God wanted me to do. I did not want to tell anyone else because I felt like they would not believe or accept it, but the message stayed with me in my heart, and it was so strong that I decided to tell my family. Sister Gladys told me that she would set a time for me to preach my first message.

Mother and Grandmother were very happy for me, and they encouraged me so much, but there were some who did not want to accept it. I was told that I could not do that. I was also told that I did not have enough education, and I also felt that I didn't, but the Lord spoke to me in my heart and said that he never told anyone to do anything that they could not do. I knew from that experience that God was my strength and my present help, and through him, I could do what he asked me to do.

6

Overcoming the Obstacles

I began preaching. Sister Gladys used me, and she helped me in every way that she could. I stayed real nervous when I would get up to preach for a long time, but as time went by, it got better. There were some people in the church who were not pleased with my preaching. One of the brothers who was there said that if I was going to preach, he was not coming to church. That hurt Mother and Grandmother real bad, and it hurt me also, but I had to overcome that. Mother and Grandmother did also. We all stayed there in church and trusted God to help us through, and he did. I am reminded of the words of Paul when he said, "Therefore I take pleasure in infirmities in reproaches in necessities in persecutions in distresses for Christ sake for when I am weak then am I strong" (2 Cor. 12:10).

Time went by. I still preached when I was asked. There was a lady in our church. She was also a minister. Her name was Katty Polly. Where she lived was a very short distance from where we lived, and she became a very good friend to me and Lee. We would get together in the evenings and pray together.

A few years went by, and the Lord revealed to Sister Gladys for her to go to another town and to start a work there. Everyone at church did not want her to go, but she had to be obedient to God. Another pastor came and filled her place at our church. We missed her so much. She began her work in a town called Murfreesboro, Tennessee. The Lord blessed her with a lot of people in her church there. We would go sometimes and visit with her.

As time went by, the Lord began to reveal to Sister Polly and to me about a work for us to begin in a very small place about six miles out of Lewisburg, and we began looking around for a building. We did not find anything for a while. Sister Polly became sick and had to be put in the hospital. I went to see her one day, and I told her that I was going to look again, and while I was driving around, I saw this little store front building. I stopped, and I went to the house next door and knocked. A lady came to the door, and I asked her who owned the little building. She said that she and her husband owned it. I asked if it was for rent, and she said that it was, and then I asked how much they were renting it for. She said $22 a week. I told her that we wanted it for a church, and I would let her know.

I went back to the hospital, and I told Sister Polly what the lady said. We talked about it, and we knew that just starting out, we could not pay that much, so we prayed. We asked the Lord if this was the place that he wanted us to have to let the lady go down on the rent. I went back and talked to the lady again, and I told her that we could not pay that much just starting out. The lady stood there and thought about it for a few minutes, and then she said $11 a week. She went down half of what she did ask.

I went back and told Sister Polly, and we knew that the Lord wanted us to have that building. We rented it, and we began to pray that God would supply everything that we needed, and he certainly did. I needed a Bible stand, and Lee's daddy built me one and brought it to the building. We needed chairs, and we didn't have the money to buy any, and the funeral home let us borrow some chairs until we could get some. It took a long time, but God made a way for us to get some pews.

Going Forth with Hard Work

We knew that it was going to be a lot of hard work just starting out with our church. I had been preaching as a helper at the other church, but now I was the pastor. Sister Polly and I would pray together a lot of nights until midnight. We wanted to see souls saved. It was just a few of us there for a while. Mother and Grandmother were very happy to be with us, and they were willing to help in every way that they could. It was amazing how God worked for us. The brother at the other church who said if I was going to preach he would not come, he came with us, and he was a great help. We began having bake sales and yard sales to help raise money for our church to pay the rent and utilities. We would make pies, and I would take them to work with me, and people there would buy them. We worked very hard, and we did it with a willing mind for God's work. The Lord began to send us more people, and we were so thankful.

Before the Lord led us to our little building while we were still at the other church, we had formed a gospel singing group. It was Lee and me and his cousin Ray and his wife, Linda. Lee played lead guitar, and Ray played bass. I had learned a lot more how to play the guitar. Lee taught me. We would go to other churches and sing on Saturday nights and sometimes on Sunday evening. We stayed busy, and we enjoyed it so much. We saw people come to the Lord and accept him in their hearts, and we also began seeing people give their lives to God. In our little church, we baptized a lot of people. The Lord blessed our work so much.

A few years went by. The sewing factory where I worked closed down, and I had to find a new job. I was a little worried about looking because I didn't know if I would be asked about my education, but the Lord was with me. I didn't have any problem getting a job. I worked different places, mostly factories. I learned real good at whatever that they put me to do. One factory was where they made pencils, and I liked it there real well, but I had to work a night shift. It was hindering me from going to church through the week. I didn't stay there very long. I learned through my commitment to God that his word teaches that "if God be first, he will meet the need" (Matt 6:33).

Our little church was doing good. I would read and study the Bible a lot. The Lord would reveal things to me. He taught me how to read and to understand so much in his word. He sent people my way many times that helped me understand more of his word. I had a great desire to learn, and I am so thankful for how God helped me. Our church had grown so much that we were pushed for room, and we found another building that was bigger. It was in town, and we moved in it. We rented it for about two or maybe three years, and the Lord made a way for us to buy it. We grew more. God blessed us so much, and he also blessed our singing group. We were still going every weekend somewhere and singing. The Lord opened doors in so many towns and places. It was such a great blessing to have the opportunity to go and be a light to people and to tell them about Jesus.

I got a job at a newspaper company. I would sell and deliver papers. I learned and did good there, and I liked my job. I worked at this for maybe two years, and there was a small restaurant in town that became available. Lee talked to the owners, and we rented it with another couple. As I mentioned earlier, I loved restaurant work. We began to work, and our business began to grow, and we were doing real good. We had good help. It had been a long time since I had worked in a restaurant, but it seemed to just come naturally for me. I was very happy with it. Lee and I had bought a house in town. God was blessing us so much. I would work every day at the restaurant. We closed on Sunday, but after about maybe six or eight months, the people who owned the restaurant sold it, and we had to let it go. The people who bought it needed help, so I went back and worked for them.

Our church was still doing good, but I still had to work. We would have fundraisers at different times to help with our church payment. A few months went by, and the business at the restaurant got a little slow for the people who bought it, and I was not getting enough hours that I needed, but the Lord blessed me. I found another job at another restaurant in town.

My children, Sharon and Sue and Regina, had got married and were doing well. They would come to church sometimes and bring my grandchildren. As several years had gone by, Sharon had three girls, Sue had two boys and one girl, and Regina had one boy. Mother and Grandmother were still real faithful to our church. Sue and Regina were also faithful coming to church, and they were called into the ministry. God used them, and they were a great help to our church. The Lord blessed, and he always supplied our needs.

We had a brother who was coming to our church. He was a minister, and he gave the church a large amount of money, and we bought new carpet for the floor. Later all the members gave love offerings. God was blessing Lee with his job, and he gave a large amount of money. We bought new pews and an altar bench. Everyone had a mind to serve the Lord and to give.

Great Favor and Blessings of God

I have learned that no one can never outgive God. The Lord blessed our church, and he blessed us to be able to work and to give. He gave us great favor. He made a way for us to buy a piano for the church and also a set of drums. We had a great sound system. We were blessed and highly favored. Sister Polly and I would go often to the church and pray, and through our prayer time, we saw results because prayer makes a difference.

Time was going by. Grandmother began to get sick. She had to go to the hospital. She had a heart condition. We did not know if she would make it, but God took over, and through his healing power, she made it. I was always real close to my grandmother, and I called out to the Lord for her. She was able to come back to church, and she would stand up and raise her hands and praise the Lord for what he did for her. Mother took real good care of her. Grandmother and Mother were real close to each other. Mother could not imagine life without Grandmother. To me, it was like I had two mothers. I loved them dearly.

More time was going by. Mother and Grandmother and my stepdad had sold the old house that they had in the country where I grew up, and they had moved to town. They were so happy to have water in the kitchen and a bathroom in the house, and they had gas heat. All this was a great help to them.

More time was going by, and in the year 1985, on April 2, Sharon was having a birthday party for one of the children. After the party was over, Grandmother became sick. Mother called me to come over, and we had to take her to the hospital. They admitted her in the hospital. She began to get worse, and after about three days, she had a stroke, and they could not do any more for her. Grandmother could not talk to us anymore. The doctor put a tube down her nose into her stomach to feed her and let her go home. I went every day to see her, and I prayed that God would heal her. Mother and all of us did all that we could for her, and on the second day of June, we were all in her room with her. I was sitting on the side of her bed holding her hand. Mother was standing at the foot of her bed. It was Sunday, at 7:20 a.m. Grandmother went home to be with Jesus. It was hard, but I had to realize that God was ready for her, and it was her time. She was healed now and doing fine. We all missed her so bad, but we had to trust the Lord to give us strength to make it, and he did.

Sister Gladys came and preached her funeral. There was an old song that Grandmother really loved, "Will There Be Any Stars in My Crown." I sang that song that day. It was hard, but I felt like that was what the Lord wanted me to do, and I know that Grandmother would have been pleased. Mother still came to church, but she had a real hard time learning to accept what had taken place. God gave her the comfort and strength she needed daily. It was just her and my stepdad in the house, and it was lonely there without Grandmother, but they made it. I would go by to see them almost every day to make sure they were all right.

Time went by, and one day in January of 1987, I received a call that something was wrong with my stepdad. I went to the house, and the ambulance had come and taken him to the hospital. When I got there, Mother was waiting to hear from him. It was not long until the doctor came out to talk with her, and he said that he was gone. There was nothing they could do. He had a massive heart attack. Mother felt that she could not make it through.

When You Can't, God Can

After everything that Mother had already gone through, now this happened. She was alone, and she didn't know what to do, but it was all in God's hands. I prayed so hard for Mother, and I began helping her in every way I could. I took her to the store and to the doctor and everywhere she needed to go. There were times she would come home with me and spend the weekend. I would take her home on Monday. Lee and I would take her out to eat, and she enjoyed being with us, but when she would get home, she would get depressed. I went every day to see about her, and I would call her at night to make sure that she was all right. Sometimes one of the grandchildren would go and see her and spend the night with her, and that would help her to have someone to talk to. She had a little dog, and he was company to her, but Mother was having a real hard time.

I was still preaching at the church, and I was also still working. We were still going and singing on the weekends. I would go and get Mother and take her with us a lot of times. She enjoyed going with us. I had to totally depend on the Lord to give me strength daily with everything I had to do. Sharon would come over to help Mother a lot of times.

As time went by, Mother began to forget to take her medicine, and sometimes she would take it and forget that she did, and she would take it again. We knew that we had to do something. I took her to one of the best hospitals in Nashville, and the doctor diagnosed her with Alzheimer's. I knew that Mother would have to have someone with her all the time, so my daughter Sharon and her family moved in the house with Mother to help and where she would not be alone. Sharon helped her with her medicine and cooked for her, but I still went every day to see about her.

7

The Stretch Began

Many times in our lives, God allows us to go through stretching experiences that prepare us for what is ahead. It is like the runner who trains to get himself prepared for the race that is ahead, but it is not easy. It is so hard to face difficult situations that come in our life; but God will stretch us until we can face and accept things that we thought we couldn't but we can, things that we think we are going to lose our minds over but we don't, things that we just know we won't make it but we do. I didn't have any idea how far God was stretching me in all the situations that had begun. I suddenly began buying vitamins and herbs that were supposed to help the memory, and I would give them to Mother. Sometimes she did not want to take them, but I insisted, and she would. As time went by, I saw very little results.

I wanted the best care for Mother. I took her back to the doctor in Nashville where they gave the diagnosis of Alzheimer's, but the medication that they wanted to give her had not been approved, and I refused her taking it. I didn't want anyone experimenting on Mother. Mother and I were close. I could not imagine life without her. I prayed. I stood on the Word. I spoke the Word. I claimed healing for her, but it got worse. I felt hopeless. I felt helpless and powerless. I had seen God heal and raise Mother up many times. She had been a diabetic, and God healed her. She had heart problems and had to have a pacemaker, and God had spared her and let her live. She had done well, but in this, my faith was being tried. In these times are when all human efforts fail. I was being stretched to the limit.

As time went by, it got worse. We would go often to a restaurant to eat, and Mother enjoyed going to eat, but she got to where she could not order for herself. I had to order for her. Sometimes her conversation would be good, and sometimes it would not be. I still prayed and looked for Mother to get better, but guess what, it still got worse. In 1993, she fell and broke her hip. I left work and took her to the doctor and from there to the hospital. The doctor said she would have to have surgery, and they said also that after she was put to sleep, the Alzheimer's would get worse, and it did.

After about a week in the hospital, we took her home. They had put a pin in her hip, and after she had been home about two weeks, the pin came loose, and back to the hospital we went. She had to have surgery again and being put to sleep again. The Alzheimer's got even worse. The doctor began giving her a medication that was for Alzheimer's while she was in the hospital, and in a few days, they came and told us that the medication was damaging her liver, and they had to stop that. I felt like the world was caving in on me. I could not picture a day without Mother. Each time that she went in for surgery, my heart was in my throat. My stomach felt like jello. I saw God bring her through and spare her life through his wonderful mercy.

She spent about two weeks in the hospital with the second surgery, and while in there, she would not eat. Her mind was so confused that she could not remember to eat. We knew that something had to be done, so the doctor said they would put a feeding tube in her stomach. When they came and took her to surgery for that, I went to the chapel there in the hospital. I got on my knees, and I begged God to not let my mother die. I stayed with her the whole time that she was in the hospital. I had to take time off from work. The people whom I worked for were tremendously understanding. We brought her home, and I saw God with his mighty hand of compassion reach out to my mother.

As time went on, she learned to walk on a walker with our help. It was one day at a time. We would sit her in a wheelchair, and she would sit for a while, and we would have to lay her down. She learned how to eat again, and that was a miracle. The doctor told us to leave the feeding tube in because we would need it later, and we did. We would take her to church, and when the singing would start, she would clap her hands. Sometimes she could understand words that we would say to her, and sometimes she could not, but what was so amazing and a wonderful blessing to me. I would quote the Lord's Prayer to her, and she could say it along with me. I would sing "Jesus Loves Me" to her, and she would sing along with me.

Mercy and Mercy Again

All these circumstances were teaching me to trust God more and to depend on his word and his faithfulness day by day. The Psalms of David said,

> They that trust in the Lord shall be as Mount Zion which cannot be removed but abideth forever as the mountains are round about Jerusalem so the Lord is round about his people from henceforth even forever. (Ps. 125:1–2)

As time went by, it was a downhill ride. There were times I would have to get up in the late night hours and go to Mother. I would drive down the road and pray all the way there for God to have mercy and let my mother live. It was back and forth to the hospital. It was like we were going around in a circle, but through all this, God was teaching me to accept the things that I could not change, and at the same time he showed me his mercy time and time again through all the sorrow of her extended illness. Every day I watched the woman who had loved me, raised me, fed me, and changed my diapers when I could not do for myself; and now I was feeding her and changing her diapers.

When the storm raged and all human efforts failed and I was sick with worry, there were times that I felt like I could not make it; but I did. I had to trust in the Lord even when I could not see anything, but by faith, I knew he was there. All this continued for a long time. Mother got worse. She had a few ministrokes, and she finally got to where she could not talk to us at all. She could not sit in her wheelchair. She just had to lie in bed, and we had to keep her turned every few hours. I knew that time was drawing nigh for her; and on October 4, 2004, Mother went home to be with Jesus. On the night before she died, I was sitting there watching her suffer, and I prayed. I told the Lord that I wanted him to heal her but just don't let her suffer, You can take her home. And that is what he did.

I still miss her and Grandmother, but God has been my help. He has been my strength because his grace is sufficient (2 Cor. 12:9) and his mercies are new every morning (Lam. 3:23). I continued to preach the gospel, and God has blessed me through everything that we all have been through. We just learned to depend upon God's word. He took care of all my family. He has kept his arms of protection around all of us. Through our heavenly Father, we survived rejection and criticism on every side but still blessed, talked about and put down but still blessed, because the Bible says, "For he saith to Moses I will have mercy on whom I will have mercy and I will have compassion on whom I will have compassion" (Rom. 9:15). It is for sure if God makes a promise, he will keep it.

I had to realize that there will always be difficult times in life, and so many of them I will not understand, but this I know: God will never make a mistake. I am sure that the blind man did not understand why he was blind. He had not committed sin, nor his parents. He had never seen his parents. He had never seen the flowers bloom. He had never seen the rain or the sunshine. Someone had to lead him everywhere he went, but when Jesus saw him, he gave him a miracle. He spat on the ground and made clay and anointed his eyes. He sent him to the pool and told him to wash, and the Bible said he came seeing saint (John 9:1–7).

My youngest daughter, Sue, was born with an abnormal bladder. She has to catheterize herself every day. She has not received her healing for that, but she was also diagnosed with MS, and God miraculously healed her. I am learning daily that I have to trust God when I don't understand. It is like the old song that says,

> Farther along we'll know all about it
> Farther along we'll understand why
> Cheer up, my brother, live in the sunshine
> We'll understand it all by and by.

I have some wonderful memories of Mother and Daddy and Grandmother. Sometimes I like to just sit down and close my eyes and reminisce about the good times we had at home. When I was a child, Daddy would build a fire in the old fireplace, and the flame would blaze so high that it would light up the room, and we would all sit around the fire at night and laugh and talk. He would tell stories about things he used to do when he was a young man. We only had one another. We didn't have friends to come by and sit and talk with us because of our family situation, but we enjoyed one another.

The Journey Was Long, but We Endured

There are many times I think of the scripture in the Bible that tells us that with God, all things are possible (Matt. 19:26). My family and I have had a long and real hard journey, but we have not traveled it alone. God has walked with us every step of the way because he promised he would never leave us nor forsake us (Heb. 13:5). There have been a lot of disappointments and a lot of pain along the journey, but I read where David said that weeping may endure for a night but joy cometh in the morning (Ps. 30:5). Now that night may seem like forever, but the Lord always comes to help us just in time.

The Bible tells about a woman who was in a meeting where Jesus was teaching. She had a spirit of infirmity for eighteen years and was bound together and could in no way lift up herself. Infirmity means to be feeble or sick or weak. Whether this was physical or mental, this woman had been plagued by this spirit for eighteen years. She was broken and could not help herself, and what she needed could only come from the hand of God. This was a long journey for her, but Jesus saw her and called her to him and said to her, "Woman thou art loose from thine infirmity." Satan had her bound, but Jesus set her free (Luke 13:11–16).

I have shed a lot of tears along this journey, but Jesus has been my friend, and he has lifted me up when my flesh felt like I could not make it. Mother and Grandmother have gone, and we know that people have to die, but spirits don't die. Their spirits still live in my heart. I miss going by to see them and talking with them, smelling the good food that they would have on the stove cooking, and sometimes taking some of it home with me. All this was like a great summer breeze. I miss them in church with me on Sundays, but God has blessed our church, and he is still blessing. He has sent people in our church who are faithful, and they know about my family situation, but it doesn't matter to them.

A lot of years have gone by, and we are still working for the Lord and seeing people saved and healed and delivered and made whole. I thank and praise God for my church family. We press daily with a determination to make it to the end.

One day I was at the hospital with my granddaughter, and I noticed a portrait hanging on the wall. It was a big heap of rocks, and in the midst of all those rocks, there were some flowers blooming. As they were coming up, out of the middle of them, written below the rocks was the word *determination*. This was a message for me that tells me that I have to have my mind firmly made up no matter what my circumstances might be. Determination is to not be weakened by the difficulties that you meet. God is still good all the time. I have learned that he walks with us and teaches us, and sometimes he carries us so the journey still goes on. We have to trust our heavenly Father for he does have greater things in store for us. We were not promised that endurance would be easy, but the Bible says that God is our refuge and strength, a very present help in trouble (Ps. 46:1).

We only receive victory when the battle is finished. There are times that fear will come our way, and it is for certain that fear will hold us back and keep us from going forward. I have had to strive to overcome the fear of rejection, but if we are going to a new level in God, we have to learn to overcome the spirit of fear. The Bible says that there is no fear in love but perfect love casteth out fear (1 John 4:18). We know that Jesus is our perfect love, and as long as we hold his hand, we can and will overcome. There are a lot of obstacles along the journey as we travel, but I have learned that I have to lay myself on God's table of mercy and say, "Lord, here I am. I can't make it on my own. I can't fix anything, but I trust you, dear Lord, to fix it all for me." He has never failed to be my help. God really does care how we feel.

8
What Happens If I Forgive

There are so many people in the world today who hold unforgiveness in their heart. Some will go on for years with this inside of them, and this is something that will destroy them. Jesus said that the thief cometh to steal, to kill, and to destroy (John 10:10), and if we allow unforgiveness to live inside of us, there will never be total victory. We cannot afford to let this happen to us. There are people who sit in church every service. Some will sing in the choir. Some are deacons. Some are on the usher board. Some will teach a class. They will raise their hands and praise the Lord. They will go up and pray with people, but they have unforgiveness in their heart against someone who hurt them.

Forgiveness is not a feeling. It is a choice. You have to make a choice to forgive. There are many times we don't feel like getting up and going to work, but we make a choice to do it, and when we reap the rewards from it, we are so glad that we did. Unforgiveness is like a slow-burning fire that keeps burning slow and keeps spreading until it totally destroys you. A lot of people will say, "But you just don't understand how that person hurt me. I really did not deserve what they did to me." But the truth is Jesus did not deserve what was done to him, but he still forgave. It is a proven fact. Statistics have proven that unforgiveness causes heart trouble and high blood pressure. We have to realize that our relationship with God can easily be hindered because of our relationship with people. Unforgiveness will control your moods and your attitudes. It has ruined relationships, homes, and ministries.

Forgive literally means to let it go and get it out of you. It has nothing to do with the other person, but it has everything to do with you and me. I have had people tell me, "I cannot forgive the person who hurt me," and that makes them a slave to that person. If that person can hinder their worship, then that's what makes them a slave to that person. Forgiveness is not a weakness. It is a strength unforgiveness is a stronghold. It is like an animal that is tied by a chain. It does not captivate all of the person, just a part of the person; and once it has a grip, it will restrict other areas. It works like a chain. When a dog is chained to a post or whatever, the chain is around his neck. It does not have his legs tied. It does not have to. It has him by the neck; and as long as it has his neck tied, it has his feet tied, the whole body is captivated in one area.

Unforgiveness is a very strong chain. It is not easily broken. It has so many people's hearts bound with bitterness and hatred, and to be free, the chain has to be broken. You have to make a choice to let it go. We were born to be free. Jesus said, "If the son therefore shall make you free ye shall be free indeed" (John 8:36). The truth is no matter what has been done to you and no matter who it was that did it, it is not worth holding all that bitterness. We want God to be merciful and forgive us, but we have no right to ask for something we're not willing to give. Jesus was alone on the cross while others stood by and watched, but he never showed any bitterness at all. He prayed, "Father, forgive them for they know not what they do," and they parted his raiment and cast lots" (Luke 23:34). It is time to get rid of it and let it go. Jesus told us how it really is in Matthew 6:14–15: "For if ye forgive men their trespasses your heavenly Father will also forgive you but if ye forgive not men their trespasses neither will your father forgive your trespasses."

Blessed When the Right Choice Is Made

I remember so well a few years before Mother passed. I mentioned earlier in this story I worked a long time in different restaurants, and as years went by, so many things changed. The drugstore that had the soda fountain where I would go with Mother and

Grandmother and get ice cream was not there anymore. A doctor and his wife owned the building, and they rented it to a lady who put a restaurant in there. It was so beautiful. The stools and the counter were still there. I went and talked with the lady about a job, and she hired me, and I worked for her for a long time. She had a big buffet, and people could help themselves. There were tables all around. It was a big place, and sometimes it would fill up with people.

Down the street from the restaurant, there was a law office. It was the office of the judge who denied me the privilege of going to school. He had got up in age, but he would walk by the restaurant every morning going to his office. At lunch, he would come in the restaurant to eat. Everyone could look at him and see that his health was not good. His hands would shake real bad. He always wore a black suit, and some of the people that I worked with there knew about my situation. They would tell me that I should tell him who I was, but I never saw the need to do that. Some of the people did not like to wait on him, and one day some of them told me, "You wait on him. We will not." My reply was "I will wait on him." I had waited on him before. I really did not mind waiting on him. He could not go to the buffet and get his own food because his hands shook so bad he would spill his food, and when he ate, he would spill it on himself. He could not help that, and I would go to his table and tell him what we had. I would ask him what he wanted, and he would tell me, and I would go to the buffet and get it and take him a plate and serve him. I felt no anger or bitterness at all because of what he did to me. I made a choice a long time ago to let it go, and when I did, it didn't hurt anymore.

Many years ago, I was working in a factory, and I was operating a machine. I caught my finger in the machine, and I had to go to the hospital and have stitches put in it. From that, it left a scar on my finger, and when I look at it, I am reminded of what happened and of the pain that I felt, but it doesn't hurt anymore. I have the inside scars, and I remember how it hurt when I was a child of what the judge did, but now it does not hurt anymore. I am so thankful that God helped me to forgive and let it go.

I AM WHAT I AM

A lot of times I think about a great story in the Bible of a man whose name was Joseph. He was one of the sons of Jacob. God was with Joseph. His father made him a coat of many colors. The Lord gave him dreams, and he gave him the gift to interpret dreams, and his brothers hated him. They were jealous of him, and the more he would tell his dreams, the more they hated him. One day his father sent him in the field to look for his brothers, and when they saw him from afar, they began to say, "We will get rid of this dreamer. We will kill him." When he got to them, they took him and stripped him of his coat of many colors, and they put him in a pit. One of the brothers said, "Let us not kill him," and they took him out of the pit and sold him to a company of Ishmeelites, and they took him down to Egypt.

Joseph suffered and went through so many trials, and he didn't do anything to deserve it, but God gave him favor. After a long period, the king of Egypt had a dream, and no one could interpret it. He called Joseph and told him that he had heard that he could interpret dreams, and he told his dream to Joseph. He did interpret the dream for him, and the king put Joseph over everything that he had. He told him that only in the throne would he be greater. He took off his ring and put it on Joseph, and he dressed him in fine linen and put a gold chain on his neck. The Bible said that seven years went by, and they were plenteous years just like the dream that the king had, and it all happened like Joseph said that it would. They had plenty of food to be laid up and saved, and then a famine began in all the land, and people began to come to Egypt to buy food.

Jacob heard the good news, and he told his sons to go down to Egypt and buy some food. They did, and when they got there, they saw Joseph, but they did not know him. Joseph knew them as he talked with them. The Bible said that Joseph remembered the dreams that he told his brothers, but he turned his face from them and wept. He gave them the food that they came for, and they paid him for it, but when they left, they found that Joseph had put their money back in their sacks. The brothers did not understand. Joseph made them leave one of his brothers with him until they went home and returned with the youngest brother, Benjamin.

Joseph was glad to see his brothers. He wanted to know about his father, Jacob. The story goes on and tells that when they got back with Benjamin, they still did not know Joseph. When Joseph saw Benjamin, he had to go to another room. He wept, then he washed his face and returned, and he began to have food prepared for them to eat. They arose and left to go home, and Joseph sent men and had them brought back. He could not reframe himself from them anymore and told everyone to go out except his brothers, and he told them he was Joseph, their brother. The Bible said that he wept aloud that everyone heard, and he told them to come near him. He said, "I am Joseph that you sold into Egypt, but God has preserved life for you and others through me." He hugged and kissed his brothers, and from there they took wagons and went to Canaan and got Jacob and all the family and came back to Egypt.

Joseph gave them all their needs, and he took care of them. Seventeen years went by, and it came time for Jacob to die, and he did. They took Jacob back to the buring place of his father, and they buried him there. Joseph's brothers said among themselves, "Joseph will now hate us, and he will begin to take revenge on us because of the evil that we did to him." They sent a messenger to Joseph saying to him, "Your father commanded before he died for you to forgive your brothers for the evil that they did to you." Joseph began to weep, and then his brothers came and fell down before him and told him they would be his servants. Joseph said to them,

> Fear not for am I in the place of God but as for you ye thought evil against me but God meant it until good to bring to past as it is this day to save much people alive now therefore fear ye not I will nourish you and your little ones and he comforted them and spake kindly unto them. (Gen. 50:19–21)

Joseph made a choice to forgive his brothers. He loved them regardless of what they did, and God turned it all around and brought good out of it. Love always wins. I like what Joseph said before the famine came. He had two sons, and when the first one was born, Joseph called him Manasseh. He said, "For God said he hath made me forget all my toil and all my father's house." The name of his second son is Ephraim. He said, "For God has caused me to be fruitful in the land of my affliction" (Gen. 41:51–52). In other words, Joseph said, "God blessed me anyway." He had to suffer and go though much pain, but God brought him through it all.

The Bible tells us in Hebrews 13:8 that Jesus Christ is the same yesterday, today, and forever. I am so thankful that he never changes. God is the same today as he was in Joseph's day. I make my choice to always forgive, because there is a release and freedom that comes with forgiveness.

9

Chosen to Serve the Lord

The Bible tells us in John 15:16, "Ye have not chosen me but I have chosen you and ordained you that ye should go and bring forth fruit and that your fruit should remain that whatsoever ye shall ask of the father in my name he may give it you." I am so glad that Jesus chose me and loved me with his unconditional love. There have been many times through the years that I have wondered why God chose me to be a part of his ministry knowing that I don't have education like other ministers, but I do know that God has a purpose for everything that he does. I have prayed so much for the Lord to give me wisdom, and I thank and praise him for everything that he has given me. He has sent so many people my way to help me, but God himself has been my best teacher. There is a song that we sing sometimes in church, and it says, "Nobody can do me like Jesus."

God has blessed me so much through the years. He has let me write some songs. I would sit down with my guitar, and he would give me the words. I had some of them recorded. I have also done a lot of evangelizing, and I really enjoy doing that, but I enjoy pastoring also. I have done a lot of Bible studies in people's homes and have prayed with them. I have also done a lot of jail ministry, and I had the privilege to go to the ladies' prison in Nashville and preach. Our singing group also went there and sang.

I have seen God work miracles so many times through prayer. We have one lady who is in our church. She is a very good friend of mine. We have known each other for many years. She came to my house one day, and she asked me to pray for her. She had a knot on the side of her nose, so we knelt down on our knees at the side of my couch, and we began to pray. She put her hand on her nose where the knot was, and she began to cry and rejoice. She said it's gone. God gave her a miracle. There was another lady in our church. God healed her from cancer and also from heart problems.

Keeping the Faith

Though the years, there have been a lot of times that it has been a struggle to hold on to my faith because there is always a voice that will come and say you can't. This voice is not from God. It is the voice of Satan. He has told me so many times, "You are not capable. You don't know how." His voice can bring a shiver of fear over you, but I have had to take a stand and say, "If God says I can, then I know that I can." The devil is a liar. The Bible says that the enemy had come and taken David and his men's families captive, and they lifted up their voice and wept until they didn't have any more power to weep, but David encouraged himself in the Lord (1 Sam. 30:1–6).

Sometimes we just have to stand still and believe, and God will never fail to come to our rescue because he is always on time. Mary and Martha thought that it was too late when Jesus finally got to their house, and they said, "Lord, if you had just been here, our brother would not have died." But it was not too late because Jesus called Lazarus back to life out of the grave (John 11). It is for sure that our faith will stand trial, but I have to constantly remind myself that with God, all things are possible (Matt. 19:26).

Many years ago, we had a lady and her children that came to our church. She was faithful. At that time, she lived across the street from where we lived. She would come over at my house sometimes and use the phone. One morning she came running over, and she said, "My house is on fire. I need to use your phone." All the time she was there, she was praising the Lord and saying, "Thank you, Jesus!" When the fire department got there, all she lost was a mattress, and everything else was all right. She held on to her faith.

We don't need faith for something we can see, but we need faith when everything is falling apart. When life doesn't make any sense at all, when a loved one dies and we wonder why that had to happen, when bad people prosper and the good suffer, when the job falls through and the marriage ends, through all these kinds of circumstances, we have to realize that God is still there; and we have to keep on running the race. Paul taught us to run with patience the race that is set before us (Heb. 12:1), but there are times that the trials and tribulations will last for so long that only God himself can give the patience that is needed through his wonderful grace.

There is a little song that a beautiful young lady used to sing in our church, and I was always blessed when I heard the words that said,

> I held on till the storm was over
> I don't claim to be a hero and I don't have all the answers
> Not because I'm great, not because I'm good, and not because I'm strong
> But I held on

I have learned that this road of life that we walk down daily gets so rough and rocky sometimes, and it feels like the pain will never stop. We learn to endure things that are mind boggling, and in these times, God will always reassure us with a word as he did for Paul. The Bible said that Paul had a thorn in his flesh, and it was something that was troubling him. He went to God about it three times, and the Lord spoke to him and said, "My grace is sufficient for thee. for my strength is made perfect in weakness" (2 Cor. 8:9).

What God Chooses Man Can't Stop

I remember a message that I preached one time, and the point was that everything is not like it looks. God chooses who he wants, and many times he picks someone who doesn't look the part, but he knows what they can be. The Bible tells us that the Lord seeth not as man seeth for man looketh on the outward appearance, but the Lord looketh on the heart (2 Sam. 16:7). God picks and uses people who in man's eyes look unworthy, but he will make them to be what he wants them to be. He calls the things that are not as though they were because he knows that he can make them become what he said they would be. Read Romans 4:17.

I am reminded of the prophet, Amos. He was a country boy. History teaches that he was born in Judah, and he was among the herdsmen of Tekoa. Tekoa is located on a hill ridge that overlooks a frightful desert wilderness that continues down to the very edge of the Dead Sea where the wild animals howl day and night. Amos was also a gatherer of sycamore fruit. These trees grow far out in the desert, so we can see that Amos was a farmer who worked hard. He didn't go to the school of ministry to receive a degree to learn how to preach the word of God, but the Lord saw something in him that man did not see. God saw something of great value inside of Amos, and he chose him and told him to go and prophesy to his people, Israel.

He sent him to Bethel, which was one of the capital cities of the northern kingdom. He gave him a message for the people. It was a message of judgment against the surrounding nations, and the people there did not want to hear what Amos had to say. He didn't look the part and didn't fit in with all those people in Bethel, but he was there to obey God. He was criticized and put down. He was ridiculed. The priest there told him to go back where he came from and prophesy there because they did not want to hear his message, but Amos took a stand for the Lord, and he said to Amaziah, the priest,

> I was no prophet, neither was I a prophet's son but I was a herdsman and a gatherer of sycamore fruit and the Lord took me as I followed the flock and he said unto me go prophesy unto my people Israel. (Amos 7:14–15)

The Lord looked far out in the desert and picked a young man to preach his word, and he gave him boldness to stand.

I remember again when I was a very young girl. I would go down the road from our house, and there were a lot of oak trees around. The little acorns would fall off them on the ground, and I would sit down on the ground and pick them up and play with them. All those years had gone by. One day I remembered sitting and playing with those little acorns, and I began to wonder if they could be used for anything. I asked someone whom I was talking to about them, and the man told me that they could be given to pigs for them to eat. I began to look and search a little more about them, and I found that a black dye of commercial value is inside the little cups that are around the acorns. This let me know that they may not look like they are worth anything, but they have value, and there is something good in them. They can be used.

The Lord picked David when he was just a young shepherd boy. He knew he could use him. David didn't look the part, and his brothers did, but God chose David to be king. The Bible says that David was a man after God's own heart (1 Sam. 13:14). When the Lord picked Paul who was Saul at that time, he was persecuting the Christian people and putting them in prison and also consenting to their death. God saw something in Paul that man did not see, and he brought him down and changed him and turned his life around. Paul began to obey God. He preached the Word, and souls were saved and healed. Paul wrote most of the New Testament.

When Jesus chose most of his disciples, he didn't go to the rich part of town to find them. One day he was walking by the seaside, and he saw Simon Peter and Andrew, his brother. They were fishing, and he called them and told them to follow him, and they did. He walked on a little farther and saw two more, and he told them to come and follow him, and they did. When the Lord chooses someone, he begins to mold them into a new vessel that he can use. Many will say they are not qualified to be a preacher or teacher, but when God gets through molding them, they are a new vessel, and they are qualified.

When a potter picks up a ball of clay, he puts it on the wheel, and he begins working on it. When he gets through with it, it is all new. It is not the same. The potter will take something that is nothing and make something out of it. That is what Jesus did for me. The Bible says that the Lord spoke to Jeremiah and told him to go down to the potter's house, and when he went, he said that the potter took the clay that was in his hands and made it another vessel. Read Jeremiah 18:1–6. Jesus is the potter, and we are the clay. He makes us into what he wants. I know that I was chosen to serve the Lord.

10
Walking Over Fear

There will be times that we all will experience the raw taste of fear, but as we go through life, we always have to learn to trust God. David said, "What time I am afraid I will trust in thee" (Ps. 56:3). David knew what troubles were. He knew what it was to have enemies to fight against him. Sometimes David would cry. Sometimes he would complain, and sometimes he would fear, but he would always pull himself together and begin to praise God and to trust him. There will always be battles in life to fight. I have had to fight many of them, but through my trust and dependence on my heavenly Father, I am still standing.

My mind goes back again to when I was a child. I was so afraid of the dark, and my grandmother would light the old kerosene lamp. She would turn the wick down low, and then she would put a piece of paper in front of it, and it would shine enough that I could see. I would lie real close to her, and that would calm my fear.

God sent an angel to Gideon while he was threshing wheat at the wine press and gave him a message that he was a mighty man of valor and that he would win the mighty battle of the enemy, which was the Midianites. Gideon was afraid, and he began to question and say, "If God is with us, where are all the miracles, and why have all these things happened?" But he moved forward and listened to God, and he won the battle just like the Lord told him that he would. Through all his fear, he trusted and obeyed his God. Read Judges 6:11–13 and chapters 7 and 9.

Moving On to Higher Levels

God has greater things in store for his people, but I have learned that it is a pressing way to receive. The Bible tells us to draw nigh to God and he will draw nigh to you (James 4:8). The way we can draw closer to God is through prayer. We have to have a prayer life. The more that we spend time in prayer, the more it will bring us into a greater relationship with him. Prayer makes a difference. It helps us to grow to a new level in God. I have listened to people talking a lot of times about how busy their day has been, and they forgot to pray, or they didn't have a lot of time. I know that time is going by, and we live today in a fast lane, and almost everyone is in a rush, but we have to press on. There has to be a time made for prayer.

I mentioned earlier in the story that I did a lot of factory work. Before I went back to work in the restaurant and after the shirt factory closed, I worked awhile in a pencil factory. After a period, someone opened a small place in town, and they made men's shirts. I went to work there, and I was doing well. Then a coat factory opened up in town, and I began to think that I would go there and try to get a job. When I went, they hired me, and I worked a few weeks. Those coats were so heavy and bulky that I was having a real hard time sewing them. I began to get weary, and I knew that I had to work, so I sat at my machine and prayed. One day I got up and went to the restroom. I got down on my knees in the floor, and I prayed and asked the Lord to make a way and give me another job. When I got home that evening, I went to my bed and laid down for a while. I was still praying, and it was not long until my phone rang. It was the supervisor from the place where I had quit, and she asked me if I wanted my job back. I knew that God had answered my prayer. I went back to work there the next day.

God answers prayers. There are so many times that I tell the people at our church, "You have to pray!" When the Lord answers prayers, it strengthens our faith. Hannah prayed. The Bible says that she wept sore. She had a sorrowful spirit. She desired a son from the Lord, and she made a vow to God that if he would give her a male child, she would give him back to him. She prayed in her heart. Her lips moved, but no one could hear her words. Eli, the priest, thought she was drunk; but Hannah began to tell him, "I have not drunk any wine nor any strong drink, but I have poured out my soul to the Lord."

Eli, the priest, said to her, "Go in peace and the God of Israel grant you your petition that you desire and asked of him." Hannah went her way, and her countenance changed, and she was not sad anymore. She knew that God was going to give her a son. The Bible says that Hannah conceived and bore a son, and she called him Samuel. The Lord remembered her, and Hannah nursed Samuel and kept him with her until he was weaned. Then she took him to the temple and gave him back to the Lord like she said she would. Read 1 Samuel 1. The Bible goes on to say that Hannah made Samuel a little coat and took it to him every year. God is a merciful God by Hannah's example of prayer. She became forever an encouragement to others to keep on praying.

It Is Wonderful to Walk in Freedom

The apostle Paul taught us, "But now being made free from sin and become servants to God Ye have your fruit unto holiness and the end everlasting life." When Jesus came into my heart so many years ago and forgave me and set me free from all my sins, it has been so great. Even though my family and I have suffered, we still have walked in freedom again. I remember back when I was a child the well that we had in our yard did not have enough water to wash clothes and to water the cows and the mules that Daddy had. There was a man who lived about a mile up the main road, and he had plenty of water on his land. He would tell Daddy to come and get what he needed. Daddy had an old wagon, and he would hitch those mules to that wagon, and he would put some big barrels in there. I would climb up in that wagon and hold on to one of those barrels, and we would go down that old rocky lane. It would shake me so bad riding over those rocks, and it would be smoother when we would get on the main road. It would take a long time to get there, and then it would take a long time to fill the barrels and go back home, but I would feel so good and so free playing around the trees and the well house while Daddy filled the barrels.

    I have some wonderful memories of my childhood, and oh yes, I can remember the sad times, but Jesus was always there. I have learned through the years that I cannot allow past circumstances to stop future opportunities. The old prophets in Hebrew 11 were not concerned about where they had been. Their minds were filled with where they were going because they were walking by faith, and they knew that what God promised he would without a doubt perform. God is good, and he is so awesome.

11
There Is a New Day Coming

I am just about to come to a close to this book, but I just cannot close it until I talk a little bit about a man in the Bible whom I have preached about, and so many times I have read about him. I am blessed over and over. His name is Mephibosheth. I thought at one time I would never learn to say his name, but one day the Lord let me hear someone say his name, and I said, "Lord, I have to remember how to say Mephibosheth." He was the grandson of Saul who was king before David. The Bible says that Mephibosheth was lame on his feet; and the reason was when he was five years old, the word came that Saul and Jonathan, his grandfather and father had died in battle. His nurse picked him up and began to run with him, and she dropped him, and he fell and became lame (2 Sam. 4:4). Mephibosheth had to suffer from the pain of being dropped.

Years went by. He grew up and became an adult, still lame and could never walk normally like other men. We can read where he was put in the house of Machir in a place called Lodebar, which was a place that means "with no communication." Mephibosheth was there with people but still alone and could not talk to anyone. His name means "ashamed."

The message of this story is that there are so many people who have been dropped and left with issues. They have scars from the pain they have been left in Lodebar, and they don't know what to do. They feel alone. They can't talk to anyone. It hurts to bad.

MARY ANN PRUITT

Something Wonderful Is About to Happen

Someone reading this can relate to what I am saying. Mephibosheth was pushed aside and left as a reject and a nobody, and he was ashamed. He had been in Lodebar for so long he felt like a nobody, but one day King David began to look around and ask some questions. He said, "Is there anyone left from the house of Saul that I may show kindness to for Jonathan's sake?"

One of Saul's servants said, "Jonathan had a son, and he is lame on his feet."

David asked, "Where is he?"

The servant told David that he was in Machir's house in Lodebar. David told him to go and fetch him out. He went and brought Mephibosheth to David, and the Bible says that he fell on his face before David and did reverence, and David told him not to fear. He said, "I am going to show you kindness for Jonathan's sake, and I am going to restore you all the land of Saul, and you are going to eat bread at my table continually." Mephibosheth then bowed before David and said, "What is thy servant that thou shouldest look upon such a dead dog as I am?" He looked at himself as a dead dog, but the king looked at him different. David told Saul's servant to go and work the land and bring in the fruit for him that he would have food.

David said, "As far as Mephibosheth, he will always eat at my table as one of the king's sons." Through all of Mephibosheth's rejections and being lame on his feet, he found favor with the king. We never read where he was ever healed. He had a problem, but he still had a seat at the king's table. When all of David's sons gathered around the table and sat down, Mephibosheth from his waist up looked the same as the others, but if they looked underneath, there was a problem, but he was still one of the king's sons. He enjoyed the royal blessings of the king.

I can truly relate to what this message says. I have been dropped and hurt. I have gone through the deserts and the wilderness down in Lodebar, but Jesus has brought me out. He is the king of kings, and I have a seat at the king's table. I have learned that if people don't like me, that it is all right. I still have a seat. I preached this message.

I AM WHAT I AM

It has been a lot of years ago, and there was a brother in our church at that time. He came to me and told me that he would never forget that message. He could relate to that so much. He has gone to be with the Lord now, but there would be times that I would see him at his work and also through a lot of sickness that he went through, and he would always say, "I have still got a seat at the king's table."

Yes, Mephibosheth had been pushed back and forgotten about, but King David showed kindness and love to him and accepted him in his family as his own son. This is a picture of what King Jesus did for me when he came to where I was and brought me out and accepted me as his child. Someone reading this can say the same. He brought you out and loved and accepted you and gave you a seat at his table. I have learned from this story that God always has a plan and a purpose for our lives.

I am reminded of Moses when he was just a baby. To keep him from being killed, his mother hid him for three months, and then she put him in an ark made of bull rushes, and she daubed it with slime and pitch. She laid him in the flags by the rivers brink, and the Bible tells us that Pharaoh's daughter went down to the river to wash herself. She looked and saw the ark, and she sent her maid to fetch it. When she opened it, she saw the child, and he wept. She had compassion on him, and then she sent and called a nurse of the Hebrew women. She was the child's mother. Pharaoh's daughter told her to nurse the child for her, and he became the son of Pharaoh's daughter. She called him Moses because she said, "I drew him out of the water" (Exod. 2:1–10).

God intended for Moses to live because he had a plan and a purpose for him. Moses became one of the greatest leaders that we read about. God used him to lead the children of Israel out of bondage and through the Red Sea in the wilderness. Moses found favor with God through his obedience. We can read in Deuteronomy 28 that blessings favor our obedience.

We Must Stand Strong

The apostle Paul told us when we have done all to stand, "Stand therefore having your loins girt about with truth and having on the breast plate of righteousness and your feet shod with the preparation of the gospel of peace" (Eph. 6:13–15). I mentioned earlier in the story about a lady who is a very good friend who came to my house for prayer, and the Lord gave her a miracle. She and her husband are members of our church. This lady has been through thick and thin, but she has always had strong faith in God to keep standing no matter what happened. When she was young, she had two children; and while they were still babies, she had to have her left arm removed because of a shot that had a dirty needle. It caused cancer, but she made it through. She had to learn to survive with one arm to do everything that she had to do and raise her children, but she had a determination like I have never seen before. It is amazing to see the things that she learned to do with one hand. Being defeated was a phrase that she never accepted. She has always stood strong with great faith, and God has blessed her and given her so many great miracles.

As we walk down life's journey, we come upon a lot of things. We see a lot of beauty along the way, and that brings joy and happiness in our hearts. But then a little farther down the journey, we meet up with a lot of pain that causes sadness and a lot of tears, and it is in these times that we have to stand still and say, "Lord, I am depending on you." Nobody likes pain, but that is a part of life. All the hurts and disappointments and failures that we face while on this journey will bring opportunities for us to know the Lord in a greater depth of his spirit and his power that will give us victory as we continue on.

There are a lot of church people today who do accept Jesus as their Savior, but they refuse to believe and to accept that he still works miracles. Some will say that when the disciples died, the miracles ended, but a disciple is a follower of Christ, and all the disciples are not dead. Jesus is still performing miracles. We just have to believe and keep our faith strong. A lot of times it is a struggle to not get weary along the way, but Paul said, "And let us not be weary in well doing for in due season we shall reap if we faint not" (Gal. 6:9).

In Moses's day, he sent people out to spy the land that had been promised to them by God, and when they came back, the ones who were afraid gave their report that they could not take the land because there were giants in the land. They said, "We are not able to go up against the people for they are stronger than we are" (Num. 13:31–32). But we have to always remember that there will always be giants along this journey; and these giants have names such as sickness, discouragement, depression, insecurity, financial problems and trouble with family. We have to stop looking at the giants and start looking at God because he is bigger and he is greater.

If we will keep our focus on God, he will always help us through all the hardships that life holds. He is the lily of the valleys (see Song 2:1), but if we never have any valleys, how can we know he is the lily? He is our deliverer, but for God to deliver us, there has to be some kind of tribulation for him to deliver us from. A lot of times our greatest victories come out of the worst and hardest trials.

12

What Happens When the Pain Doesn't End

I am about to conclude the story. It has taken me a long time to write this book, but while writing, there have been a lot of things that have happened. I talked in the seventh chapter about how God will stretch us to make us ready for what is ahead, and I experienced that stretch through the loss of Grandmother and Mother. Little did I know what would take place next as years went by.

In the year 2006, my husband, Lee, had a stroke in his right arm and leg. He had to go to the nursing home for a while, but God miraculously brought him through, and he was able to go back to church and play his guitar and sing. Two years later, in 2008, my daughter Sharon suffered a heart attack and had to have a stent; but through God's mercy, she was all right. Then in 2010, she had another heart attack and had to be life flighted to Nashville to the hospital; and while in the hospital, she had a third heart attack and had to have more stents. She also had to be put on dialysis, but God spared her life. He brought her through.

The next year, 2011, my husband's mother became very sick. She had to be taken to the hospital, and from there she was taken to the nursing home. She was eighty-nine, and she had lived a real good life. She was a prayer warrior, and she lived close to the Lord. She would sit in her chair and read her Bible for hours without stopping. She was a good God-fearing woman. She had lived with us from the year 1983.

In the year 1982, my husband's daddy became sick, and he passed away. It was a sudden thing, and it brought so much pain to all of our family. My husband had a very hard time when that happened, but through God's great mercy and strength, he made it. His mother had lived with us for twenty-eight years, and while she was in the nursing home, she went home to be with the Lord. This brought so much pain to all of us. I preached her funeral, and it was very hard, but God gave me strength.

In that same year, my daughter Sharon had another heart attack. That was the fourth one, and this time she died for ten minutes. The paramedics worked with her and got her heart beating again. We gave God praise because we knew it was him who brought her back to us. She spent a very long time in the hospital and also in the nursing home, and in the year 2012, she had to come live with us. She could not walk without help from someone. We were having a very hard time, but I was still preaching and telling people that with God, all things are possible.

Time was going by, and in the same year 2012, our daughter Regina noticed a lump in her breast, and she was told later it was cancer. She had to have both breasts removed, and then she had reconstructive surgery. She suffered so much through that, but through God's great mercy, she made it through.

Time went by, and in the year 2017, my husband, Lee, suffered another stroke. He was taken to the hospital, and from there, he had to go to the nursing home. After a few days in there, he suffered another stroke, and he had to go back to the hospital in the critical care. We called out to the Lord for him, and God came on the scene with his healing power. My husband began to recover. He had to go back to the nursing home for a while, and the Lord helped him to be able to come home, but the strokes affected his speech. He was not able to carry on a good conversation with anyone. He took speech therapy, but it did not help, but we were so thankful that God had brought him through and that he was home and doing as well as he was.

MARY ANN PRUITT

The Pain Got Worse

In that same year, Regina began to have some more problems, and she became very sick and had to go to the hospital. She had a lot of fluid buildup that affected her breathing. The doctors did not know at the beginning what it was, but they decided to send her to Nashville to St. Thomas Hospital. There they found that the cancer had come back, and it had spread all through her body. We did not know what to do. All we could do was to pray and trust God. This news brought much pain to all of our family. She came home, and it was not very long until her pain became so bad that it was unbearable. Soon she had to be taken back to the hospital, but I want to tell about a wonderful miracle that God did for her before she became at her worse.

In her sickness, she had prayed and asked the Lord to let her have a granddaughter and to let her get to go to Israel. Her son Josh and his wife had three boys, and Regina loved and cherished those grandsons. The church she was attending had a group that was going to take a trip to Israel, and God blessed her and her husband, David, to get to go with them. Her daughter-in-law became pregnant and gave birth to a beautiful baby girl. God answered her prayers.

We did not know at the time, but her time was drawing nigh. While she was in the hospital, all the family was there. It was Friday morning. I went to her bed and leaned down, and I said to her, "I don't want you to go." She said to me in a very weak voice, "Mama, I've got a home in heaven." I could not say anything else because she was ready to cross over and be free from all the pain. We all stayed with her, and on Sunday morning, she went home with Jesus. There is a beautiful song that she loved, and she had requested for that song to be sung at her funeral. The name of it is "It Is Well with My Soul." We learned at the time that she went home with the Lord that a sister in her church was singing "It Is Well with My Soul." This brought extreme pain upon all of us, but we know that God doesn't make any mistakes, so we had to trust God for his help and go on. We did not know then, but there was more pain on the way.

Double Pain

Six months went by. One Monday morning in April 2018, Lee became real sick. It was about 5:00 a.m. He got up, and I got up with him. I told him that he probably had a stomach virus. As he sat in his chair in our living room, I could tell that his breathing was getting bad. I began to pray, and I called out to the Lord. I then called 911, and they came and took him to the hospital. I was there with him. I began calling the church people for them to pray. His body went into septic shock, and he could not talk to us. The church people came to the hospital and prayed. We did not know what was wrong, but they found he had *E. coli* bacteria that got in his bloodstream.

We all stayed with him, and we prayed with all our hearts for him. We sang to him. We talked to him. I begged the Lord to heal him and let him live. The doctors tried all kinds of antibiotics, but nothing helped. I could not imagine going on in life without Lee. We had been together for fifty-two years. I sat at the side of his bed and talked to him. The nurse told me that he could hear, but he could not speak. On Wednesday morning, we were all there with him, and he went home to be with the Lord. Only God could let anyone know how bad my pain was, and again, we did not know then, but God was not through.

Triple Pain

A little less than three months went by. It was in July. One Friday morning, everything seemed to be normal. Sharon would always have breakfast and lie back down and take a nap before getting dressed to go to dialysis, but this morning was different. When she woke up and she sat up on the side of the bed, someone always had to help her get dressed, and before that could happen, her right arm had what they called a fistula in it. That is what they did dialysis in. Her arm started bleeding, and all of a sudden that fistula burst; 911 was called, and they came and took her to the ER. She had lost so much blood that her heart stopped.

I had been praying all the way to the hospital. The church people were praying. My daughter Sue was there with me. The doctor would not let us back there where Sharon was, but it was not long until the doctor came to where we were and told us that they did all that they could do, but they could not bring her back. We were all in shock. The pain had not stopped from losing Regina and Lee. I was at the breaking point. I felt like my pain was more than I could bear. Within nine months, I had lost three, but I had to look up and say God is good. I don't understand, and I may never understand, but I still have to say, "Praise the Lord."

I cried day and night. My tears were uncontrollable. I faced sleepless nights. I asked the question why, but then I thought of David, and I have to say as he said, "I will sing unto the Lord as long as I live. I will sing praise to my God while I have my being" (Ps. 104:33). God always knows best. There will be a lot of times in life that things will happen that are not fair, and it will bring pain, but we have to just trust God. He will always be there for us. Even though things are not like what we want them to be, the pain has not stopped for me, but Jesus is my strength. I will keep on trusting him.

There is a beautiful song that we used to sing, and it says, "Through it all I learned to trust in Jesus. I learned to trust in God. I learned to depend upon his word." Job was a great man of God, and he lost all his family and also all his possessions, but he still trusted God. The Bible tells us that Job said, "All the while my breath is in me and the spirit of God is in my nostrils my lips shall not speak wickedness nor my tongue utter deceit God forbid that I should justify you till I die I will not remove mine integrity from me my righteousness I hold fast and will not let it go my heart shall not reproach me so long as I live" (Job 27:3–5). Job lost everything, but he held on to God, and because he was faithful, God blessed him with double.

I lost a husband and two daughters, but I am thankful for what I still have. I have still got one daughter, and I have grandchildren and great-grandchildren and also great-great-grandchildren. I love them all very much. I am still preaching the Word. Our church is small, but the spirit of God is still in the house. We are seeing people healed and needs are being met. I am still blessed. I can say again, as David said,

> In my distress I cried unto the Lord and he heard me. (Ps. 120:1)

> I will lift up mine eyes unto the hills from whence cometh my help my help cometh from the Lord which made heaven and earth. (Ps. 121:1–2)

So what happens or what do we do when the pain doesn't end? We just keep on trusting because God will never fail.

One More Thing

I would like to say, as Columbo used to say in his TV program, there is just one more thing. My prayer is as you read this story, you would just give God praise and know that through everything that we all went through, it was God who was right there holding us up and leading us through. Before I started to write this story, I met and talked with a lady who writes a lot of poetry. She has also written a number of books. I told her that I would like to find someone to write a book about my life and my family, and I began to tell her about my story. I told her that I did not know how to write it, and she told me and encouraged me to write it myself. She said, "If you get someone else to write it, it will not be you." She added, "You write and tell it in your own words." So I decided to begin.

I have prayed all the way through for the Lord to help me and give me wisdom and understanding. I stopped while in town one day in front of the building where the restroom was that I was not allowed to use it when I was a little girl. It is a historic site now, and I read the sign that tells about it. My mind went back to those days, but I thank and praise God because he has brought me from a mighty long way. I chose a long time ago to forgive and let it go. I have been put down, and I have been let down. I have been slapped down, and I have been thrown down, but Romans 8:31 says, "What shall we then say to these things? If God be for us who can be against us?"

If you are hurting and going through something that you feel like you cannot make it through, just hold on and take courage because Jesus is on the way. He is always on time. He has come and rescued me so many times in life when it was like I was in a dry and barren land, alone with nothing. That is why I can say as Paul said, "But by the grace of God I am what I am" (1 Cor. 15:10).

I AM WHAT I AM

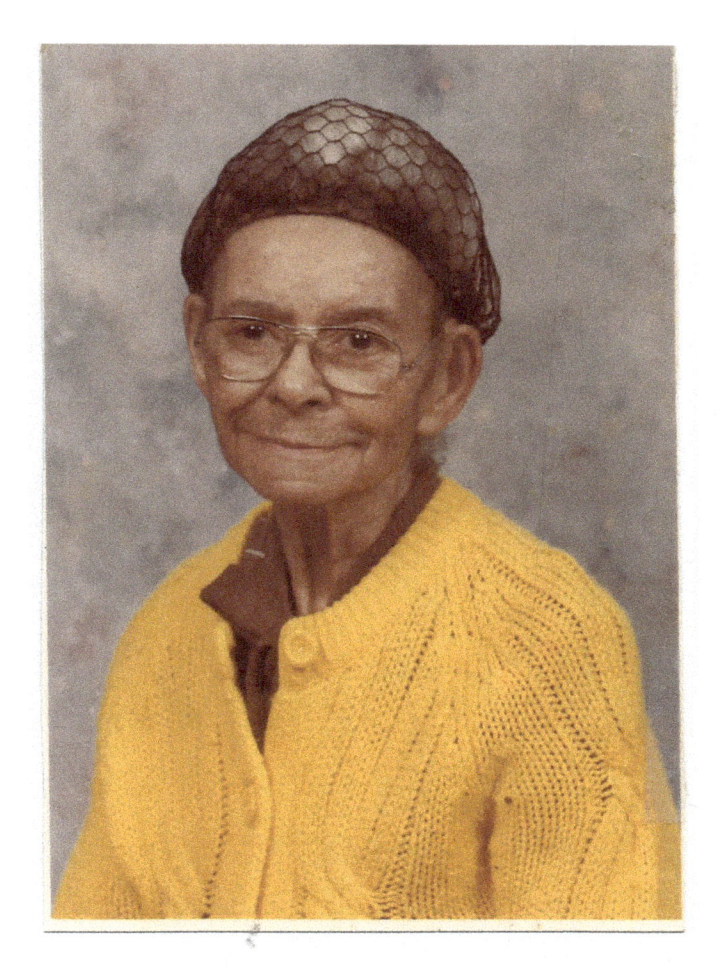

Miss Mary

MARY ANN PRUITT

Mary Ann @ age 18

Mary Ann age 20

I AM WHAT I AM

Ann Anderson

Dock Anderson

Mary washing clothes from a fire kettle

WASH DAY (SERIES 1) NO. 57200858. A PICTURE FROM THE HOYT WAKEFIELD ALBUM OF PASSING SCENES. THE WASHTUB, WASHBOARD AND THE BIG IRON KETTLE WERE ESSENTIAL TO THE WEEKLY WASH UNTIL THE APPEARANCE OF THE WASHING MACHINE WHICH CAME IN A MAN OPERATED FORM AROUND THE 1920'S.

MARY ANN PRUITT

I AM WHAT I AM

Maryann & Mother Ethel

The Ole House

Mary on Front Porch

85

MARY ANN PRUITT

Ethel when she was a baby

I AM WHAT I AM

Mary Pruitt

Bo Joel Josh Tammy

Tela Wendy Lydia

Maryann's granchildren

Maryann's greatgrandchildren

I AM WHAT I AM

Miss Ann & Mary

MARY ANN PRUITT

Mary Ann Age 11

Mary Ann

Mary Anderson
Mary Anns Grandmother

I AM WHAT I AM

David & Sue McCool
Maryanns daughter

David & Regina Black
Maryanns Daughter

Sharon & Randy Martin
Maryanns daughter

Lee & Maryann Pruitt
Mother of Sue, Sharon, Regina

Mary Ann Pruitt age 50

Mary Ann Pruitt present

This is the old house that Mary, Ethel and Mary Ann lived.

This is the old school house where Mary and Ethel would have went had they been accepted.

I AM WHAT I AM

Regina Black
Mary Anns Daughter

Sharon Martin
Mary Anns Daughter

IN MEMORY OF SHARON, Regina, Lee, Reva

Reva Pruitt
Lee's Mother

Lee Pruitt
Mary Anns Husband

MARY ANN PRUITT

Ethel & Maryann

Ethel & Her Husband Ed

Ethel Outside Playing gutair

Ethel

I AM WHAT I AM

Ethel Curry
Miss Marys Daughter

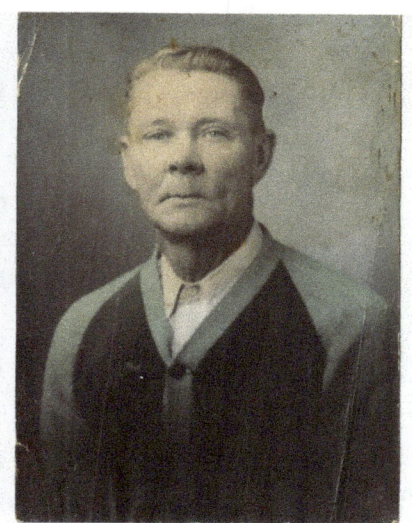

Ernest Ethels Father

About the Author

Mary Ann Pruitt was born on April 20, 1942, in the small town of Lewisburg, Tennessee. Her parents were Edd and Ethel Craig Eakes. At the age of eleven, she got to know the Lord Jesus Christ as her Savior, and she learned about the great power of God. She gives him the glory and praise. He helped her overcome all her childhood traumas and heartaches. She was denied going to school, along with her mother and grandmother who were denied the same privilege, but through God's great love and mercy, they made it through.

Mary Ann became an ordained minister in 1968. She has been singing from about the age of five. She got married to Lee Pruitt in 1966. They were married for fifty-two years before he went home to be with the Lord. She had two daughters, Sharon and Regina, who have also gone home to be with the Lord. She has another daughter, named Sue, who lives in Lewisburg, Tennessee. Mary also has seven grandchildren, eleven great-grandchildren, and eleven great-great-grandchildren. She pastors a church in Lewisburg, Tennessee, and she lives in Shelbyville, Tennessee. She still enjoys singing the old hymns that tell about Jesus. She has also written a lot of songs, and some of them she has recorded.